Golf
GREATS

AL BARKOW
DAVE BARRETT

PUBLICATIONS INTERNATIONAL, LTD.

Al Barkow is editor-at-large of *Golf Illustrated* and the former editor-in-chief of *Golf Illustrated* and *Golf*. He is the author of *Golf's Golden Grind: A History of the Tournament* and *Gettin' to the Dance Floor: An Oral History of American Golf*. He was a contributing writer to *20th Century Golf Chronicle*, *Golf Legends of All Time*, and *Wit & Wisdom of Golf*.

David Barrett is a senior editor at *Golf*. He was a contributing writer to *20th Century Golf Chronicle*, *Golf Legends of All Time*, *Wit & Wisdom of Golf*, *Golf in America: The First One Hundred Years*, and *The PGA Championship: 1916–1984*.

Cover photos: **Allsport USA:** David Cannon *(left & bottom)*; Jamie Squire *(right)*.

All rights reserved under International and Pan American copyright conventions. Copyright © 1998 Publications International, Ltd. This publication may not be reproduced or quoted in whole or in part by any means whatsoever without written permission from Louis Weber, C.E.O. of Publications International, Ltd., 7373 N. Cicero Avenue, Lincolnwood, Illinois 60646. Permission is never granted for commercial purposes. Printed in U.S.A.

CONTENTS

INTRODUCTION • 7
AMY ALCOTT • 10
WILLIE ANDERSON • 12
TOMMY ARMOUR • 14
JOHN BALL • 16
SEVE BALLESTEROS • 18
JIM BARNES • 22
PATTY BERG • 24
TOMMY BOLT • 28
JULIUS BOROS • 30
PAT BRADLEY • 32
JAMES BRAID • 34
JACK BURKE JR. • 36
DONNA CAPONI • 38
JOANNE GUNDERSON CARNER • 40
BILLY CASPER • 42
GLENNA COLLETT VARE • 46
HARRY COOPER • 48
HENRY COTTON • 50
FRED COUPLES • 52
BEN CRENSHAW • 54
JOHN DALY • 56
BETH DANIEL • 58
JIMMY DEMARET • 60

- Roberto De Vicenzo • 64
- Leo Diegel • 66
- Chick Evans • 68
- Nick Faldo • 72
- Johnny Farrell • 76
- Jim Ferrier • 78
- Raymond Floyd • 80
- Doug Ford • 84
- Hubert Green • 86
- Ralph Guldahl • 88
- Walter Hagen • 90
- Sandra Haynie • 96
- Harold Hilton • 98
- Ben Hogan • 100
- Hale Irwin • 106
- Tony Jacklin • 108
- Bobby Jones • 110
- Robert Trent Jones • 116
- Betsy King • 118
- Tom Kite • 120
- Bernhard Langer • 122
- Tony Lema • 124
- Lawson Little • 126
- Gene Littler • 128
- Bobby Locke • 130
- Nancy Lopez • 132

Lloyd Mangrum • 136
Carol Mann • 138
John McDermott • 140
Bill Mehlhorn • 142
Cary Middlecoff • 144
Johnny Miller • 148
Old Tom and Young Tom Morris • 152
Byron Nelson • 154
Larry Nelson • 160
Jack Nicklaus • 162
Greg Norman • 168
Francis Ouimet • 172
Arnold Palmer • 176
Corey Pavin • 182
Henry Picard • 184
Gary Player • 186
Nick Price • 190
Judy Rankin • 192
Betsy Rawls • 194
Johnny Revolta • 196
Chi Chi Rodriguez • 198
Donald James Ross • 200
Paul Runyan • 202
Doug Sanders • 204
Gene Sarazen • 206
Patty Sheehan • 210

DENNY SHUTE • 212
CHARLIE SIFFORD • 214
HORTON SMITH • 216
MACDONALD SMITH • 218
SAM SNEAD • 220
JAN STEPHENSON • 226
CURTIS STRANGE • 228
LOUISE SUGGS • 230
JOHN H. TAYLOR • 232
PETER THOMSON • 234
JEROME TRAVERS • 236
WALTER TRAVIS • 238
LEE TREVINO • 240
HARRY VARDON • 244
KEN VENTURI • 248
LANNY WADKINS • 250
ART WALL • 252
TOM WATSON • 254
TOM WEISKOPF • 258
JOYCE WETHERED • 260
KATHY WHITWORTH • 262
CRAIG WOOD • 266
TIGER WOODS • 268
MICKEY WRIGHT • 272
BABE DIDRIKSON ZAHARIAS • 276
HISTORICAL RECORDS • 280

INTRODUCTION

○ ○ ○

BEN HOGAN, 16 months removed from a horrific auto accident that ravaged his body, was now on the verge of winning the 1950 U.S. Open. He led by three strokes with seven holes to play. However, his still-damaged legs throbbed in pain, and after his tee shot at the 12th hole, he nearly fell.

Hogan hobbled toward Harry Radix, a friend nearby. "Let me hang onto you, Harry," Ben said. "My God, I don't think I can finish."

Hogan limped through the next six holes, and by the 18th tee he had fallen back into a tie. Somehow, he needed to muster a heroic approach shot to keep his hopes alive... and he did just that. Stroking a 1-iron, Hogan launched a majestic shot that settled safely on the green. In agony, he two-putted for a tie. The next day, he prevailed in an 18-hole playoff.

It was the stuff legends are made of.

It is also one of the many captivating stories you'll find in *Golf Greats,* a book that honors the 100 greatest golfers who ever picked up a club. *Golf Greats* focuses mostly on PGA Tour greats, but the whole spectrum of golfdom is covered: LPGA stars, foreign golfers, course designers, and oft-forgotten pioneers. The roots of golf dig so wide and deep that even Scotland's Old Tom Morris, who whacked a featherie ball in the 1840s, earned a place in these pages.

The biographies in *Golf Greats* are all-encompassing, chronicling the golfers' lives from their early years through the lengths of their careers. Yet the profiles go well beyond the facts. The biographies explore the golfers' personalities, recount their fascinating personal stories, and relive their greatest golfing heroics.

The personalities of the 100 greats run the gamut, from the terse and demure to the chatty and jolly. Prior to tournament golf, Babe Zaharias performed on vaudeville, tap-dancing and playing the harmonica. Walter Hagen, though, was golf's ultimate showman. So brazen was "Sir Walter" that he sometimes sent his caddie 150 yards ahead to pull the flagstick. Then there was Bobby Locke. The stately South African so annoyed American players in the 1940s that they called him "Muffin Face." The jowly Locke dressed in knickers, a white cap, and white shoes and strolled deliberately down the golf course as he pontificated about his next stroke. When a reporter would ask him a question that was instructional in nature, Locke boldly requested $100 for his response.

Somewhere in the lives of these golfers lie compelling personal stories—sometimes comic, sometimes tragic. Lee Trevino grew up in a house with no electricity or running water, yet he was able to scrape together needed money through his golf skills and wild imagination. Trevino hustled golfers with a Dr Pepper bottle, hitting shots with the fat end and pool-cueing putts with the thin end. Young Tom Morris remains golf's saddest story. Old Tom's son won four British Opens by age 21, but he died three years later. Morris never recovered from the shocking death of his wife and baby, who both died during childbirth.

When it comes to heroic golf shots, few could match the wallop of Gene Sarazen at the 1935 Masters. Down three strokes to Craig Wood with four holes to play, Sarazen erased the entire deficit with one swing of a 4-wood, as his second shot on the par-5, 485-yard 15th rocketed to the green and then glided softly into the cup. Sarazen won in a playoff the next day. As for famous hot streaks, Byron Nelson blazed the trail with his 11 straight victories in 1945. His streak included the spectacular—he won the Iron Lung Open with a Tour-record 263 total—as well as the dramatic—he birdied five of the last six holes to win the Philadelphia Inquirer Invitational by one stroke.

If you want to learn about Seve Ballesteros's miracle shot from the parking lot, or Sammy Snead's sourpuss uncle, then spend some time with *Golf Greats*. Every star has a story to tell.

AMY ALCOTT

○ ○ ○

It took Amy Alcott only three tournaments to prove that she made the right decision in joining the LPGA Tour just six months after she finished high school. In her third event, she won the 1975 Orange Blossom Classic a day after her 19th birthday. A year and a half earlier, the Southern California girl had won the U.S. Girls Junior Championship.

Over the next couple of decades, Alcott became one of the LPGA's top shot-makers and most confident players. She won at least one tournament in each of her first 12 years on the LPGA Tour, a record for the start of a career, and captured four events each in 1979, '80, and '84. Alcott has claimed five major titles—the Nabisco Dinah Shore in 1983, '88, and '91, the Peter Jackson Classic in 1979, and the U.S. Women's Open in 1980.

Alcott turned in her finest performance in the 1980 U.S. Women's Open. She survived the heat in Nashville, Tennessee, to post a then-record 72-hole total of 280 to win the tournament by a whopping nine strokes. She had another impressive showing in the 1991 Nabisco Dinah Shore, setting a 72-hole record of 273 to defeat runner-up Dottie Mochrie by a commanding eight-stroke margin.

Alcott's best years were 1979 and 1980, when she scored a total of eight wins and ranked third on the money list each year. She was never the LPGA Player of the Year, but she won the Vare Trophy for low scoring average in 1980 at 71.51. Alcott ranked among the top 10 money winners 11 times, including nine years in a row from 1978 to '86. After her first winless season in 1987, Alcott came back to claim the Nabisco Dinah Shore in 1988, and was so happy she took a swim in the pond fronting the 18th green to celebrate. She repeated that escapade in 1991 when she won the Nabisco Dinah Shore again, but she has had little reason to celebrate since. Alcott has remained stuck on 29 victories, leaving her one short of qualifying for the LPGA Hall of Fame. Should she win the LPGA Championship, she would join Pat Bradley as the only winners of the four modern majors.

CAREER HIGHLIGHTS

Earnings: $3,135,772
LPGA Tour Victories: 29
Achievements: Won 1983, 1988, and 1991 Nabisco Dinah Shores; 1980 U.S. Women's Open; 1979 Peter Jackson Classic. Won four Tour events each in 1979, 1980, and 1984. Registered 15 top-10 finishes in 1988. Vare Trophy winner in 1980.

WILLIE ANDERSON

○ ○ ○

IT IS DIFFICULT TO ASSESS Willie Anderson's stature among the greats of the game. He competed when golf was in its infancy in America, with relatively primitive equipment and course conditioning, so it's pointless to compare scores. But one thing is certain: He was the first dominant player in American golf.

There were only two significant tournaments in the United States when Anderson played at the turn of the century, the U.S. Open and Western Open, and he won each event four times. His total of four U.S. Open titles has been matched only by Bobby Jones, Ben Hogan, and Jack Nicklaus, and has not been surpassed. Anderson is the only player ever to have won three straight Opens, claiming the title from 1903 through 1905. His 73 in 1903 and 72 in 1904 established 18-hole Open records. He finished in the top five in 11 Opens, a record that only Nicklaus has tied. Anderson's victory in the 1908 Western Open established a standard course scoring record of 288 with rounds of 71, 73, 72, and 72.

Anderson emigrated to the U.S. at the age of 17 along with his father, who was a greenkeeper in

North Berwick, Scotland. Willie took a club job in Rhode Island, the first of 10 clubs he would work for in his 14 years in America.

The slightly built Anderson was an accurate player, but his strength on the course was considered to be his calm demeanor. This served him well in 1901 when he won his first Open at Myopia Hunt Club in Massachusetts. He trailed by five strokes with five holes remaining in a playoff against Alex Smith before finishing with five straight 4s to win by one.

Anderson finished fifth in the Open in 1902, but the next year at Baltusrol's original course in New Jersey, he claimed his second title, again in a playoff (beating David Brown). He won the 1904 Open at Glen View outside Chicago by shooting his record 72 in the final round, then nipped Alex Smith again at Myopia in 1905. Anderson played in five more Opens but never again finished better than fourth. His death in 1910 came suddenly; he played three 36-hole matches the week before.

CAREER HIGHLIGHTS

Achievements: Won 1901, 1903, 1904, and 1905 U.S. Opens; 1902, 1904, 1908, and 1909 Western Opens. Became the first and is one of four golfers ever to have captured the U.S. Open four times, and is the only man to win it three times consecutively. Member of PGA/World Golf Hall of Fame.

TOMMY ARMOUR

○ ○ ○

HAD THE MASTERS STARTED before he turned 39, Tommy Armour might have achieved the modern Grand Slam of winning all four professional major events. As it was, the man known as the "Silver Scot" settled for victories in the U.S. Open, PGA Championship, and British Open, all of them in dramatic fashion.

Armour was born in Edinburgh, Scotland, in 1895 and lost sight in one eye while fighting in World War I. He emigrated to the United States after coming over to play in the Walker Cup Matches in 1922, and he turned pro in 1924. His timing was good—the pro tour was just then developing, with most of the events taking place in the winter when the pros could get away from their club jobs.

Armour's first big victory came in the 1927 U.S. Open at Oakmont thanks to a heroic finish. He played the last six holes in 2-under-par, and he birdied the 72nd hole by hitting a 3-iron to within 10 feet of the hole to tie Harry Cooper. The magnificent stroke helped earn Armour a reputation as one of the finest iron players in the game. He won the 18-hole playoff by coming from two strokes down with six holes to play, robbing Cooper of a major he would never win.

In the 1930 PGA Championship, Armour defeated Gene Sarazen, one of the top players of the day, in the 36-hole final match when he holed a 12-foot putt for par on the last hole and Sarazen missed from 10 feet. But the title that meant the most to Armour came the next year when he won the British Open at Carnoustie in his native Scotland. He trailed by five strokes entering the final round, but he stormed home with a 71 for a winning 296 total.

Shortly thereafter, the once-unflappable Armour began to have trouble holing short putts and invented the term "the yips" to describe his affliction. He ended his career with 24 professional victories. In his later years, Armour became one of the most well-known—and high-priced—golf teachers in America. His book *How to Play Your Best Golf All the Time* is considered an instruction classic.

CAREER HIGHLIGHTS
PGA Tour Victories: 24
Achievements: Won 1927 U.S. Open; 1930 PGA Championship; 1931 British Open; 1929 Western Open; 1927 Canadian Open. Captured seven Tour events in 1927. Member of PGA/World Golf Hall of Fame. Also considered one of golf's greatest teachers.

JOHN BALL

○ ○ ○

IF NOT FOR THE INCOMPARABLE Bobby Jones, England's John Ball would be considered the greatest amateur golfer of all time. In a career spanning the 19th and 20th centuries, Ball racked up eight victories in the British Amateur, the most titles captured by any player in a single major championship. The first of those titles came in 1888 and the last in 1912, mirroring Jack Nicklaus's modern feat of winning major championships over a 24-year span.

It is difficult to compare Ball's record with the records of those who came later, or even with contemporaries Harry Vardon, John H. Taylor, and James Braid, who ruled the professional game during the same period. But esteemed golf writer Bernard Darwin, who saw all the greats of the first part of the 20th century, wrote, "I have derived greater aesthetic and emotional pleasure from watching John Ball than from any other spectacle in any other game."

Ball enjoyed one great moment against the professionals. He won the 1890 British Open at Prestwick in Scotland, becoming the first Englishman to claim that title. He also won the British Amateur that year; he and Jones are the only two players to sweep those titles in the same year. Ball nearly repeated the feat in 1892 when he finished second in the British Open after winning the third of his Amateurs.

Ball was born in 1861 in Hoylake, England, where his father owned the Royal Hotel. The hotel was near the Royal Liverpool Golf Club, where Ball learned the game. In the first British Amateur in 1885, held at Royal Liverpool, Ball beat his father, 4 & 2, in the third round before losing in the semifinals.

Ball's first British Amateur title came at Prestwick in 1888. His other titles followed in 1890, '92, '94, '99, 1907, '10, and '12. The last of those victories came at age 51. In the 1899 final, Ball came from five down to beat Freddie Tait in 37 holes. Ball missed three years of competition (he served in the Boer War) before coming back to claim his last three titles. He played his last British Amateur in 1921, at the age of 60, making it to the fifth round.

CAREER HIGHLIGHTS
Achievements: Won 1890 British Open and eight British Amateur titles between 1888 and 1912, the most wins by one player in a single major championship. Played successful championship golf for 45 years, winning his last British Amateur at age 51. Is one of two players (along with Bobby Jones) to win British Open and Amateur in same year. Member of PGA/World Golf Hall of Fame.

SEVE BALLESTEROS

○ ○ ○

SEVE BALLESTEROS DASHED ONTO the golf scene with all the flair of the great matadors of his native Spain. Like the bullfighters, Ballesteros often flirted with danger.

Those who witnessed it will never forget the 1979 British Open at England's Royal Lytham and St. Annes. The 22-year-old Ballesteros, tall and slender, darkly handsome, was swinging his driver with reckless abandon, and the ball was responding accordingly, flying every which way but straight. With his driver, he would hit only eight fairways through the four rounds. One was not expected to win any championship with such wildness off the tee—especially not at Royal Lytham, notorious for its narrow, oddly angled fairways and severe rough. But Ballesteros's counter was an extraordinary talent for recovery around the greens; he was a brilliant pitcher, chipper, sand bunker player, and putter from in close.

At the start of the last round, Ballesteros was two strokes behind Hale Irwin and only one ahead of Jack Nicklaus, both far more conservative players and far more experienced in championship play. Ballesteros took no heed, and he took the lead after the 2nd hole with a birdie and a par. At the 6th, he hooked his drive a full 90 yards off-line, into the 14th fairway. His second shot went 50 yards through the green. He got his par. Continuing to play more often than not from the rough, he held his lead going into the back nine. It was at the 16th, though, where his reputation was made for all time. On the 353-yard par-4, Ballesteros drove 30 yards off-line to the right and into a parking area for television production vans. From there, he wedged to within 14 feet of the hole and made the putt that in short time ensured his victory. He was dubbed "The Car Park Champion."

The flamboyant, emotional Ballesteros was one of the most popular players on both sides of the Atlantic.

Seve Ballesteros was born in 1957 in Pedrena, a small town in rural northern Spain. His father was a farm laborer who worked in fields near the golf course where Seve caddied and learned to play. He began to play early, at around age seven, following the lead of his older brother, Manuel, who would also become a golf professional. To say Ballesteros played golf in those earliest years is not quite the word. He had come into possession of a 3-iron, the only club he would own for a year or so. And, of course, the young farm worker's boy was not allowed to play on the only course within many miles, a private club. He would earn that right in time, when his talent would be recognized far and wide.

Until then, these deprivations would turn out to be of great benefit. Seve would play every imaginable shot with that 3-iron—low ones, high ones, draws, fades, hooks, and slices, hitting the ball out of deep grass in a farm field, off hard dirt roads, out of sand. He often played his shots to tomato cans he sunk into the ground at the back of his modest home. Ballesteros would acknowledge years later that the versatility of his game, with all clubs, was born in those days with his lone 3-iron as his companion.

Because of his humble origins, a higher education was not in the cards for Ballesteros. His skill at golf was apparent while he was in his teens, and at the age of 17 he turned professional. A scant two years later, having gained some experience playing on the European Tour—and winning once—Ballesteros finished in a tie for second with Nicklaus in the 1976 British Open won by Johnny Miller. It was a stunning achievement for someone with so little seasoning at that level of competitive golf.

Seve liked the taste of it, and with what everyone came to know as soaring self-confidence, Ballesteros became a major factor on the European circuit and finally worldwide. From 1976 through 1978, he won 11 tournaments—10 in Europe and one in the United States (the 1978 Greensboro Open). Thus, in winning the 1979 British Open, he didn't in fact become a star overnight. It just seemed that way, because for the first time he was on a major stage, playing in the oldest championship in golf, and on international television.

Through 1996, Ballesteros had won at least 60 tournaments around the world, including three British Opens. Nine of those victories came on the U.S. PGA Tour, two of them in the Masters. He was also a potent figure in the revival of interest in the Ryder Cup Matches. Seve played on the European team nine times from 1979 through 1997. He served as captain for the 1997 Matches in his native Spain (Valderrama) in which Europe was victorious over the U.S. And while with his play he won more than enough points for his side, it was as much his spirited, even emotional ardor for the competition that spurred the success of his teams.

CAREER HIGHLIGHTS

Earnings: $1,550,322
PGA Tour Victories: 6
Achievements: Won 1980 and 1983 Masters; 1979, 1984, and 1988 British Opens; 1981 Australian PGA. Winner of 72 tournaments worldwide, including Open championships of nine countries and 54 events on the PGA European Tour. Veteran of nine European Ryder Cup teams between 1979 and 1997, captaining the 1997 squad in his native Spain.

JIM BARNES

○ ○ ○

Standing 6'3", Long Jim Barnes towered over most of the golfers of his day. He also was one of the best players in the game in the period just before and after World War I, winning all of what were then considered major championships (the U.S., British, and Western Opens and the PGA Championship).

Barnes was born in 1887 in Cornwall, England, where he became an assistant professional at age 15. He emigrated to America four years later, though he retained his English citizenship. Barnes was a quiet and gentlemanly man who let his golf clubs do the talking and often walked the course with blades of grass or a sprig of clover clenched in his teeth.

Barnes's greatest performance came in the 1921 U.S. Open at Columbia Country Club in Chevy Chase, Maryland. He led by three strokes after the opening day and extended his margin after each round to four, seven, and then nine strokes at the finish—the biggest victory margin this century. Barnes opened the tournament with a round of 69 and followed with 75, 73, and 72 to pull away from the field. He was serenaded up the 18th fairway by a Marine band and is the only Open champion ever to receive the trophy from the President of the United States, with Warren Harding doing the honors.

Barnes also has the distinction of winning the first two PGA Championships ever held, in 1916 and then in 1919 after a two-year gap due to World War I. He edged Jock Hutchison in the first one when he holed a five-foot putt on the 36th hole and Hutchison missed from the same distance to give Barnes a 1-up win. Barnes whipped Fred McLeod, 6 & 5, in 1919.

Although the pro tour consisted of only a few scattered events each year in Barnes's day, he is credited with 20 wins in the U.S. These include the 1914, '17, and '19 Western Opens. He capped his career by winning the 1925 British Open, considered somewhat of a surprise since he had not played particularly well in the previous couple of years. He came from five strokes back to win, taking advantage of Macdonald Smith's collapse in the final round at Prestwick. Barnes recorded a final-round 74 while Smith limped weakly home in 82 shots.

CAREER HIGHLIGHTS
PGA Tour Victories: 20
Achievements: Won 1921 U.S. Open; 1916 and 1919 PGA Championships; 1925 British Open; 1914, 1917, and 1919 Western Opens. His nine-stroke winning margin in the U.S. Open is the largest this century. Member of PGA/World Golf Hall of Fame.

PATTY BERG

○ ○ ○

SHE CAME FROM A MOST UNLIKELY region of the United States to become a great golfer, but that was the way of Minnesotan Patricia Jane "Patty" Berg. She was not daunted by any obstacles thrown her way.

Born in 1918, Berg began her athletic career as a speed skater, competing in national events. When she was 13, she began swinging a golf club in her backyard. Noting her interest in this game, Berg's father, a member of the Interlachen Country Club (where Bobby Jones won one of his Grand Slam victories, the 1930 U.S. Open), sent his youngest daughter for instruction with the club pro. Not long after, she started taking lessons from Lester Bolstad, the University of Minnesota golf coach who would work with Berg for the next 40 years. At 15, Berg entered the Minneapolis City Ladies championship and shot a 122 in the qualifying round. The next year in the same event, she won the qualifying medal and the tournament.

With that, her father began entering Patty in important national amateur tournaments and taking the family to Florida for at least a month every winter. In 1935, Patty reached the finals of the U.S. Women's Amateur championship. She would win that title in 1938, and in all would capture

28 amateur championships over a period of seven years. She played on two U.S. Curtis Cup teams, in 1936 and 1938.

In 1939, on her way to defending one of her amateur titles, Berg met with the first of a number of serious physical problems. She had an emergency appendectomy that hospitalized her for a month and essentially ended her competitive season. In 1941, while driving from Texas to Tennessee to play an exhibition to raise funds for British War Relief, the car in which she was driving with fellow pro Helen Dettweiler was hit. Berg's left knee was broken in three places, and she ended up with 75 percent use of the leg in terms of bending it. After taking therapy with a prizefighter named Tommy Littleton, she returned to the golfing wars.

A powerful, accurate driver, Berg won 57 professional tournaments despite a series of debilitating injuries.

Berg turned professional in 1940. She wasn't the first woman golf pro, but she was among the first 10. At the time, women professionals usually did not give lessons and were relegated to administrative jobs. What's more, there were very few tournaments for women pros. When Berg became a pro, there were only a handful of tournaments in which she could play, with total purse money around $500. But in the face of such a dismal situation, Berg persisted. She earned most of her income giving exhibitions and clinics for the Wilson Sporting Goods Company, with whom she signed a contract upon turning pro. In her lifetime, the short, stocky Berg would give some 10,000 clinics all over the country, all of them with characteristic high spirits and enthusiasm. She was one of women's golf's most energetic and effective ambassadors.

Patty also did something about the competitive circumstances for women pros. After serving in the Marine Corps during World War II (Lieutenant Berg worked as a recruitment officer), she embarked on creating a pro tournament circuit for women on which she would become one of its early stars. Berg was instrumental in reorganizing the Women's Professional Golf Association. The word "Women's" was changed to "Ladies" (LPGA), Fred Corcoran was hired to book events and promote them, and the Wilson Company was prompted to put up administrative costs for the first six years. Berg was the LPGA's first president. With the foundation of the circuit set, Berg went out and played.

Berg had won six times before the LPGA was formed, and from 1948 through 1962 she captured 44 more titles with a game that featured brilliant shot-making with fairway woods and outstanding putting. Her victories included the first U.S. Women's Open, in 1946, which was then played at match play; seven Western Opens; and seven Titleholders Championships. Her last professional victory came in the Muskogee Civitan Open in 1962, when she was 44 years old.

Hip replacement surgery forced Berg to end her professional playing career in 1980, but as always she continued giving exhibitions and clinics with her usual zest until she was well into her 70s—and that despite cancer surgery in 1971, major hip surgery in 1980, and back surgery in 1989. Nothing, it seemed, could keep Patty Berg down.

Of course, Berg won numerous awards in honor of her long work in and for golf. She was inducted into at least 10 Halls of Fame. She was one of the first four inductees to the LPGA's Hall and one of the first two women inducted into the PGA/World Golf Hall of Fame. She also won the 1963 Bob Jones Award, one of the USGA's highest honors. And just to remind everyone that she was as much a player as a teacher and promoter of golf, in 1991, at the age of 73, she made a hole-in-one.

CAREER HIGHLIGHTS

Earnings: $190,760
LPGA Tour Victories: 57
Achievements: Won 1941, 1943, 1948, 1951, 1955, 1957, and 1958 Western Opens; 1946 U.S. Women's Open; 1937, 1938, 1939, 1948, 1953, 1955, and 1957 Titleholders Championships. Vare Trophy winner in 1953, 1955, and 1956. Served as first LPGA president from 1949 to 1952. Member of PGA/World Golf Hall of Fame and LPGA Hall of Fame. Led Tour in earnings in 1954, 1955, and 1957. Recorded ace at age 73.

Tommy Bolt

○ ○ ○

He might be more famous for his temper than for his ability, but Tommy Bolt was one of the best golfers of the 1950s. His finest hour came at the 1958 U.S. Open at Oklahoma's Southern Hills, where he displayed an uncommonly serene temperament while beating a young Gary Player by four strokes to take his only major championship.

Bolt didn't join the PGA Tour for good until 1951, at age 33. He learned the game as a teenage caddie in Shreveport, Louisiana. After dropping out of high school to become a carpenter, Bolt competed in local amateur events. After a stint in the service, he went back to carpentry. He made brief flings at the Tour in 1946 and 1950. Finally, after spending a year as a driving-range pro, Bolt hit the Tour to stay. He won his first tournament, the North and South Open, in 1951, and was on his way. His 15 PGA Tour victories all came in an 11-year span.

The opinionated Bolt was great copy for sportswriters, and his volatile personality made him entertaining for spectators to watch. Stories of "Terrible Tommy" breaking or throwing clubs are legion. Many are apocryphal, but some are true. At the 1960 U.S. Open, Bolt hit his ball into the lake on the 18th hole at Cherry Hills, then threw his driver in, too. A young boy dashed from behind the ropes, jumped into the water, and retrieved the driver. A smiling Bolt went up to the boy to reclaim the club, but the youngster bolted, hopped a fence, and was gone with his prize.

Bolt, a U.S. Ryder Cup player in 1957, was one of the game's best shot-makers, able to bend the ball left-to-right or right-to-left at will. He was also capable of low scoring. He shot a 60 on his way to winning the 1954 Insurance City Open and opened with rounds of 64 and 62 in taking the Virginia Beach Open the same year. He won his last tournament in 1961, but as late as 1971, Bolt finished third in the PGA Championship at age 52.

Bolt also fared extremely well in Senior events. He won five consecutive National Senior Association Opens beginning in 1968. He also captured the 1969 U.S. PGA Seniors title and Senior events in Great Britain and Australia.

CAREER HIGHLIGHTS
Earnings: $320,792
PGA Tour Victories: 15
Achievements: Won 1958 U.S. Open; 1969 PGA Seniors. Finished third in 1952 Masters and 1971 PGA Championship, the latter at age 52. Captured National Senior Association Open five times in a row beginning in 1968. Member of 1957 U.S. Ryder Cup team.

JULIUS BOROS

○ ○ ○

His easygoing manner was matched by a casually elegant swing. But while Julius Boros came to the golf course with the air of a man heading to his local fishing hole to spend a relaxing day, he was always at his best in the game's biggest events, particularly the U.S. Open. Boros won the U.S. Open twice, in 1952 and 1963, and his 11 top-10 finishes in the event trail only the great Jack Nicklaus, Ben Hogan, and Arnold Palmer since World War II.

Boros was an accountant in Connecticut until he turned pro in 1950 at the age of 30. Despite the late start, he went on to have a long career, sustaining a high standard of play into his late 40s and even his 50s. He is the oldest man to have won a major title, capturing the 1968 PGA Championship at age 48. He ranked among the top five money winners at 47 and 48. And in 1975, at age 55, he lost the Westchester Classic in a sudden-death playoff.

Boros's first of 18 PGA Tour victories came in the 1952 U.S. Open at the Northwood Club in Dallas, where he posted a 68 in the third round and won by four strokes. Boros also won the World Championship of Golf in 1952 and again in 1955, leading the money list in those years.

Boros had his ups and downs over the next several years, but he hit a high note at the 1963 U.S. Open. He birdied two of the final three holes of regulation to reach a playoff at The Country Club in Brookline, Massachusetts, then fired a 70 to beat Arnold Palmer and Jacky Cupit. Boros also beat out Palmer in the 1968 PGA Championship, shooting a closing 69 to win by one stroke.

Boros was a Ryder Cup player four times, and in 1967 he became the second-oldest U.S. player ever chosen. He won the U.S. PGA Seniors in 1971 and 1977, but lost in the World Seniors each time.

Though the Senior Tour came along a little late for Boros, he played a role in getting it off the ground. He teamed with Roberto De Vicenzo to beat Tommy Bolt and Art Wall in a six-hole playoff at the 1979 Legends of Golf, an event generally credited with spawning the Senior Tour the next year.

CAREER HIGHLIGHTS
Earnings: $1,004,861
PGA Tour Victories: 18
Achievements: Won 1952 and 1963 U.S. Opens; 1968 PGA Championship. Oldest to win a major, taking the 1968 PGA at 48. Finished among the top 10 in the U.S. Open 11 times. Led Tour in earnings in 1952 and 1955. Tour Player of the Year in 1952 and 1963. Member of PGA/World Golf Hall of Fame.

Pat Bradley

○ ○ ○

SHE HAS BEEN ONE OF THE MOST consistent LPGA players over the last couple of decades on the LPGA Tour, but Pat Bradley made her biggest impact on the game with one glorious year. In 1986, she won three of the LPGA's four major championships: the Nabisco Dinah Shore, LPGA Championship, and the du Maurier Classic, failing to capture only the U.S. Women's Open. The only two other LPGA players to win three majors in a year were Babe Zaharias in 1950 and Mickey Wright in 1961. Bradley has claimed six majors in all and is the only player to have won all four of the "modern" LPGA majors, having claimed the U.S. Women's Open in 1981 (she also won the du Maurier in 1980 and '85).

Bradley grew up in Westford, Massachusetts, where she was an avid skier, but she worked hard on her golf game at Florida International University and joined the LPGA Tour in 1974. Her first win came two years later. The high point of the first decade of her career came in the 1981 U.S. Women's Open when she shot a final-round 66 to outduel Beth Daniel and win by one stroke at La Grange Country Club.

Until 1986, it appeared that Bradley was destined to be known more for coming close than for winning. She entered that year with 16 wins, but 35 runner-up finishes. She had finished in the top four on the money list six times, but never in first place. Nor had she ever won the Player of the Year Award or the Vare Trophy for low scoring average. Bradley swept those awards in 1986 when she had five wins and six seconds, then repeated the feat in 1991 when she won four times.

Bradley's career took a downturn in 1988 when she was diagnosed with hyperthyroidism. But, after taking time off to treat the condition, one of the game's most intense competitors came back determined to reach 30 wins and qualify for the LPGA Hall of Fame. She accomplished her goal by winning eight times from 1989 through 1991. Bradley added a 31st win in 1995 and has more than $5 million in career earnings. She was only the second LPGA player to reach that milestone.

CAREER HIGHLIGHTS
Earnings: $5,141,019
LPGA Tour Victories: 31
Achievements: Won 1980 Peter Jackson Classic; 1981 U.S. Women's Open; 1980, 1985, and 1986 du Maurier Classic; 1986 Nabisco Dinah Shore; 1986 LPGA Championship. Is the only woman to win all four modern majors. Led Tour in earnings and won Vare Trophy in 1986 and 1991. Member of LPGA Hall of Fame.

JAMES BRAID

◦ ◦ ◦

BY THE TURN OF THE 20TH century, golf had expanded well beyond the borders of its Scottish birthplace and was catching on rapidly in England and the United States. Indeed, two of the Great Triumvirate who dominated the British Open in the 20 years before World War I, Harry Vardon and John H. Taylor, were Englishmen. The third, James Braid, was a Scot, the son of a humble Elie plowman. But even Braid went to England to embark on his golf career, heading to London to become an apprentice clubmaker in 1893 at the age of 23.

A tall man, Braid was a long hitter for his day. Early golf historian Horace Hutchinson wrote that Braid swung with "a divine fury." Nonetheless, it took him a while to harness his considerable skills, and he was the last of the Great Triumvirate to win a British Open. Braid played in his first Open in 1894. In 1895, he began to make a name for himself by halving a match with Taylor, the 1894 and '95 Open champion.

Braid finished second in the Open in 1897, then in 1899 finished fifth to begin an incredible streak. For 14 straight Opens, Braid was never out of the top five, a feat that has never been matched (Jack Nicklaus is the next best at 11 from 1970 through 1980). Braid also had 17 consecutive top-10s, starting in 1896, matching Taylor for the all-time record.

Braid's Open victories came in 1901 at Muirfield, 1905 at St. Andrews, 1906 at Muirfield, 1908 at Prestwick, and 1910 at St. Andrews. The latter win made him the first to win five Opens, though Taylor later matched the total and Vardon reached six. Braid was the first player to shoot a round in the 60s in the Open, carding a 69 in the third round at Royal St. George's in 1904. His 72-hole record of 291 set in 1908 stood for 19 years.

Braid's record in the British Matchplay Championship is another testament to his skill. He won the inaugural event in 1903, and by 1907 he had taken three of the first five. He was victorious again in 1911; only Dai Rees in 1950 and Peter Thomson in 1967 joined him in winning a fourth.

For the last 45 years of his life, until he died in 1950, Braid was the head professional at Walton Heath, near London. He recorded a round of 74 on his 78th birthday.

CAREER HIGHLIGHTS
Achievements: Won 1901, 1905, 1906, 1908, and 1910 British Opens, becoming the first to win his country's championship five times. Also won four British Matchplay titles. Finished in the British Open top five 14 consecutive years and its top 10 17 times in a row. Member of PGA/World Golf Hall of Fame.

JACK BURKE JR.

○ ○ ○

THE SON OF A GOLF PROFESSIONAL who finished second in the 1920 U.S. Open, Jack Burke Jr. surpassed his father's accomplishments by winning 17 times on the PGA Tour.

Burke served in the Marines and worked as a club pro before joining the Tour in 1950. His finest years were 1952 and 1956. In 1952, he won four tournaments in a row—the Texas, Houston, Baton Rouge, and St. Petersburg Opens—a feat surpassed by only Byron Nelson (11 wins) and Ben Hogan (six) in PGA Tour history. Shortly thereafter, Burke finished second to Sam Snead at the Masters, thanks to a final-round 69 in windy weather. Burke won the Vardon Trophy for low scoring average that year and also led all Tour players with five victories.

In 1956, the native Texan again demonstrated his ability to play in the wind. He came from eight strokes behind to win the Masters over amateur Ken Venturi, shooting a 71 to Venturi's 80. The win still stands as a tournament record for the biggest deficit overcome in the final round. Burke also showed his comeback ability in winning the PGA Championship the same year. He was five down after 14 holes in the 36-hole semifinal at Boston's Blue Hill Country Club before defeating Ed Furgol on the first extra hole, and three down after 19 holes before rallying to beat Ted Kroll in the final. His two major titles earned him PGA Player of the Year honors.

Burke was on all five Ryder Cup teams from 1951 to '59 and posted a 7–1 record. His only loss came in a singles match in 1957, when he was the playing captain and the U.S. suffered its only postwar defeat until 1985. Burke later got some revenge when he captained the U.S. to a 1973 victory.

Burke injured his wrist in the late 1950s, and while he continued to enjoy success for a few more years, the injury eventually forced him to retire from competition after posting his last professional victory in 1963. By then, Jimmy Demaret and he were involved in developing Champions Golf Club near Houston, which hosted the 1969 U.S. Open.

CAREER HIGHLIGHTS

Earnings: $260,746
PGA Tour Victories: 17
Achievements: Won 1956 Masters; 1956 PGA Championship. Vardon Trophy winner in 1952. Tour Player of the Year in 1956. Won four consecutive events and tied for Tour lead with five total wins in 1952. Ryder Cup regular who captained U.S. teams in 1957 and 1973.

DONNA CAPONI

○ ○ ○

ONLY TWO PLAYERS HAVE WON all four tournaments that the LPGA currently designates major championships—Pat Bradley and Donna Caponi. But while Bradley's feat is recognized in Tour record books, Caponi can't officially make that claim because her wins in the 1976 Peter Jackson Classic and 1980 Colgate Dinah Shore Winner's Circle came before those tournaments received major designation. She won the two biggest majors, the U.S. Women's Open and LPGA Championship, twice each.

In fact, Caponi made the 1969 U.S. Women's Open her first career victory at the age of 24. She had learned the game from her father, a golf professional in the Los Angeles area, and joined the Tour in 1965. She finished 10th on the money list in 1968 but was winless until scoring a dramatic Women's Open triumph. Tied for the lead, Caponi had to wait out a 15-minute lightning delay before playing the 18th hole. She birdied it to shoot a 69 and win by one stroke. The next year, Caponi became the second player to win back-to-back U.S. Women's Opens (Mickey Wright was the first). She won her LPGA Championships in 1979 and '81, getting a birdie on the final hole to win by one stroke in the latter year.

Caponi never won the money title, nor was she Player of the Year. However, she was consistently among the top players on the LPGA Tour from 1969 to '81. She finished among the top five money winners seven times (second in 1976 and '80) and scored all 24 of her career victories in that span. Ten of those wins came in 1980–81; five in each year (plus an unofficial win each year with Kathy Whitworth in the Portland Ping Team Championship). In 1981, Caponi became the third LPGA player to pass the $1 million mark in career earnings. Her winning days ended abruptly after those two big seasons. Caponi remained among the top 30 money winners the next three years and among the top 60 for three more, but she couldn't find the winner's circle again before retiring in 1989. Caponi remains popular as a network television golf analyst.

CAREER HIGHLIGHTS
Earnings: $1,387,920
LPGA Tour Victories: 24
Achievements: Won 1969 and 1970 U.S. Women's Opens; 1979 and 1981 LPGA Championships; 1976 Peter Jackson Classic. Finished second in 1980 Tour earnings. One of 13 players to record first Tour win at U.S. Women's Open. Has enjoyed successful career as television golf analyst.

JoAnne Gunderson Carner

○ ○ ○

Of the great players to come along in the post–World War II era, JoAnne Carner is the only one, male or female, who nearly remained a career amateur. Not joining the pro circuit until age 30, Carner won five U.S. Women's Amateur championships, a total second to only Glenna Collett Vare. She then went on to compile a pro record that placed her in the LPGA Hall of Fame. Carner, née Gunderson, is the only player to have claimed the U.S. Girls' Junior, Women's Amateur, and Women's Open titles. She won the junior championship in 1956, also reaching the final of the Women's Amateur that year at age 17. She went on to claim the amateur title in 1957, '60, '62, '66, and '68. In 1969, she won the Burdine's Invitational on the LPGA Tour; she's still the last amateur to win an LPGA event.

With prize money rising in the pro game and no worlds left to conquer in amateur golf, Carner decided to turn pro in 1970. The former "Great Gundy" earned a new nickname on Tour when her fellow pros tabbed her "Big Momma," mainly for her ability to launch the ball long distances. Carner's gregarious personality and go-for-broke style quickly made her a popular figure in the professional ranks.

Despite an aversion to practice, Carner compiled an impressive record on the Tour, winning the Vare Trophy for low scoring average five times, earning three Player of the Year Awards, and claiming three money titles. Her biggest victories came in the 1971 and '76 U.S. Women's Opens. From 1974 to 1983, she ranked among the top five money winners in all but one year.

Despite her late start, Carner had a long stay near the top of the LPGA because she achieved more success after age 40 than any player of either sex ever has. Of her 42 LPGA Tour victories, 19 of them came in her 40s, and she led the money list when she was 43 and 44. She is the oldest player to win an LPGA event, having claimed the Safeco Classic at age 46.

CAREER HIGHLIGHTS

Earnings: $2,878,105
LPGA Tour Victories: 42
Achievements: Won 1971 and 1976 U.S. Women's Open. Won five U.S. Amateur titles from 1957 to 1968. In 1969, won last LPGA title by an amateur. Vare Trophy winner in 1974, 1975, 1981, 1982, and 1983. Three-time Player of the Year and three-time earnings leader. Member of LPGA Hall of Fame and PGA/World Golf Hall of Fame.

BILLY CASPER

◦ ◦ ◦

BILLY CASPER WAS NEVER RECOGNIZED for the golfer he was. It's difficult to say just why. It may have been the way he presented himself to the golfing public when he was in his prime. Perhaps, too, it was because he defeated one of the game's most beloved icons, Arnold Palmer, for a national championship.

In any case, from 1954, when he turned pro, through 1979, his last year on the regular PGA Tour, Casper won 51 tournaments to place sixth on the all-time winners list. His victories included two U.S. Opens (1959 and 1966) and a Masters (1970). He played on eight U.S. Ryder Cup teams, was a nonplaying captain for one other, and won the annual Vardon Trophy for low stroke average five times. He was twice the Tour's leading money winner, and in 1970 he became the second golfer in history to win more than $1 million in career prize money. He was twice the PGA Player of the Year and is a member of the PGA/World Golf Hall of Fame. By all accounts, he was one of the best players in American golf history.

William Earl Casper Jr. was born in San Diego in 1931. He was an early product of an outstanding junior golf program in his hometown, but he played his first golf, he once recalled, "over the rocky ground of my grandfather's ranch in New Mexico. It was very rudimentary, to say the least. In fact, it wasn't really a golf course at all." He entered his first tournament as a 13-year-old in San Diego. "It was during World War II," he said. "I entered as a 24 handicap and shot an 80. My entry fee was refunded. I just had a hot round, but the officials wouldn't buy that."

Casper was renowned nearly as much for his girth as his golf game. "I have a furniture problem," he said late in his career. "My chest has fallen into my drawers."

Casper attended the University of Notre Dame for a year, then opted to play professional tournament golf. He joined the PGA Tour in 1954, and two years later he won his first event, the Labatt Open. From 1957 to '71, he won at least once every year, and usually was a multiple winner. His best season in that regard was in 1968, when he won six times on the circuit and became the first player to surpass $200,000 in single-season earnings. What's more, he would win 12 times on the Senior PGA Tour from 1982 through '89, including a U.S. Senior Open in 1983.

In assessing his career, Casper once said he would have been more popular had he not tried to emulate the unemotional, stoic demeanor of Ben

Hogan. In private, Casper was a sharp-witted individual with the guile of a pool-hall sharpie. Indeed, he was an excellent pool player as a young man, a skill that transferred to his golf via an exceptional, even uncanny, ability to putt. In this he was unique. At address, his left hand rested against his left thigh and didn't go beyond it in the follow-through. The technique kept him from flipping his hands and resulted in a short, compact "pop" stroke that was highly effective for a long time. His putting skills helped him capture the 1970 Masters. Playing in an 18-hole Monday playoff with Gene Littler, Casper totaled six one-putt greens on Augusta National's front nine to open up a five-stroke lead. He prevailed 69–74 for his first and only green jacket.

Casper's game from tee to green was distinguished by a slide into impact that seemed less than graceful, but perhaps only because he was always rather heavyset. Even as a young man, Casper was constantly fighting a weight problem, and at one point he became known more for an exotic diet of health foods than for his splendid game. Perhaps, too, his weight was off-putting to the galleries.

Furthermore, upon examining his life outside of golf, he found it wanting in purpose and decided to join the Mormon church. Hence, a certain piety was added to his demeanor both on and off the golf course.

But Casper's cardinal sin, as many seemed to consider it, was when, in 1966, he came from seven strokes behind with nine holes left to play to tie Palmer for the U.S. Open, played at the Olympic Club in San Francisco. Then, in the 18-hole playoff, Casper erased a two-stroke deficit with eight holes to play to claim his second U.S. Open title. To be sure, Palmer played poorly on the back nine in both instances, but what people failed to take note of was that all the while Casper was shooting sensational scores—a 3-under-par 32 on the back nine of the championship proper and a 1-under-par 34 on that same nine in the playoff. Had he defeated anyone besides the immensely popular Palmer, Casper might have been extolled more for his great achievement. In a sense, Casper could be considered the victim of someone else's charisma.

CAREER HIGHLIGHTS

Earnings: $1,691,583 (PGA); $1,690,795 (SR)

Tour Victories: 51 (PGA); 8 (SR)

Achievements: Won 1959 and 1966 U.S. Opens; 1970 Masters; 1983 U.S. Senior Open. PGA Player of the Year in 1966 and 1970. Vardon Trophy winner in 1960, 1963, 1965, 1966, and 1968. First player to surpass $200,000 in single-season PGA Tour earnings. Member of eight U.S. Ryder Cup teams between 1961 and 1975 and nonplaying captain in 1979. Member of PGA/World Golf Hall of Fame.

Glenna Collett Vare

○ ○ ○

A CONTEMPORARY OF BOBBY JONES, Glenna Collett Vare dominated women's amateur golf in the United States much the same way Jones did the men's game. Her enduring legacy is a record six U.S. Women's Amateur titles—this in a time when women's professional golf didn't exist. And, like Jones, she was an attractive champion who always conducted herself with class.

Collett was born in 1903 (one year after Jones) and played baseball in her youth before being introduced to golf at age 13 by her mother, who thought it a more appropriate game for a girl. She came under the wing of Scottish pro Alex Smith, a two-time U.S. Open champion who reputedly said, "If I can't make a champion out of her, I'll be a disgrace to the Smith family."

Vare was perhaps the longest hitter women's golf had ever seen. Asked later how she was able to outdrive her contemporaries, she said, "Very simple. I just hit the ball harder than they did." Collett won her first Women's Amateur in 1922. After a tough semifinal loss in 1924 (her semifinal opponent's winning putt on the first extra hole bounced off Collett's ball and into the hole), she claimed her second title in 1925.

In 1928, Collett began a streak that saw her win 19 consecutive matches in the U.S. Women's Amateur, carrying her to titles in 1928, '29, and '30; she lost in the final in '31. Collett also was runner-up in 1932. Oddly, she lost the '32 final to Virginia Van Wie, 10 & 8, even though she had defeated Van Wie by a then-record margin, 13 & 12, in 1928. Collett Vare, who married in 1931, won her sixth Women's Amateur in 1935, beating 17-year-old Patty Berg in the final.

Collett Vare won the Eastern Amateur and the North and South Amateur six times each, but the one big title she never claimed was the Ladies' British Open Amateur. She reached the tournament's final twice, losing in a memorable match to British great Joyce Wethered in 1929 and falling to relative unknown Diana Fishwick the following year.

CAREER HIGHLIGHTS

Achievements: Won 1922, 1925, 1928, 1929, 1930, and 1935 U.S. Women's Amateur Championships. Captured Eastern Amateur and North and South Amateur six times each. Namesake of Vare Trophy, given annually to the LPGA Tour player with lowest scoring average. Member of LPGA Hall of Fame and World Golf Hall of Fame.

HARRY COOPER

○ ○ ○

He finished with 31 official PGA Tour victories, but Harry Cooper might be most remembered for his near misses in the game's biggest events. Indeed, he has the most victories of any player who never won a major championship (and ranks 13th on the all-time win list). Twice he completed his final round as an apparent winner of the U.S. Open, but both times the tournament was snatched away by a later finisher in what became a frustrating trend for Cooper.

Cooper was born in England in 1904, the son of a golf professional, but his family moved to Texas when he was a boy. He burst into the pro ranks quickly, winning the 1926 Los Angeles Open at the age of 21 and earning the nickname "Lighthorse Harry" because he played so quickly. Cooper's first U.S. Open chance came in 1927 at Oakmont. He three-putted the 71st hole from eight feet but still would have won outright if Tommy Armour, finishing an hour later, hadn't birdied the 18th hole to force a playoff. The 18-hole playoff was tied until Cooper took two strokes to escape a bunker and double-bogied the 16th hole.

In 1936, Cooper finished the U.S. Open at Baltusrol with what would have been a record total of 284, despite bogeys on two of the last five holes. He was congratulated on his victory, but unheralded Tony Manero was in the process of burning up the course on the way to a closing 67 for a winning total of 282.

Cooper led through each of the first three rounds in the 1936 Masters, but he closed with a 76 and finished second to Horton Smith. He was also the runner-up in 1938 at August National to Henry Picard. He never advanced past the semifinals of the PGA Championship and never returned to the isle of his birth to play in the British Open.

His second-place finishes notwithstanding, Cooper was one of the finest players of his generation. His best year was 1937, when he won eight tournaments, led the money list, and won the first Vardon Trophy. He captured the Canadian Open in 1932 and 1937.

CAREER HIGHLIGHTS

Earnings: $76,000
PGA Tour Victories: 31
Achievements: Finished second in 1936 and 1938 Masters; 1927 and 1936 U.S. Opens. Won 1932 and 1937 Canadian Opens. Won eight events, led Tour in earnings and was awarded inaugural Vardon Trophy in 1937. Member of PGA/World Golf Hall of Fame.

HENRY COTTON

○ ○ ○

THE GLORY DAYS OF BRITISH GOLF seemed to have passed when Henry Cotton arrived on the scene in the 1930s. Once the sole province of Britain's Great Triumvirate (Harry Vardon, John H. Taylor, and James Braid), the British Open had been claimed by players from the United States in every year from 1924 to 1933. But Cotton became a British hero by claiming the title three times—in 1934, '37, and '48.

Cotton, born in 1907, was one of the game's first great practicers, along with his near contemporary in the United States, Ben Hogan. Cotton came from a well-to-do family, but he hit so many balls as a young man that his hands were often blistered, and he walked with a tilt due to spending so much time with his right shoulder lower than his left in the golf stance. He became a very straight driver of the ball, much like Hogan and Byron Nelson, and had a sound all-around game, though his putting was sometimes suspect.

Cotton broke through at the 1934 British Open at Royal St. George's. He opened with rounds of 67 and 65, phenomenal scoring for that era, and opened a nine-stroke lead (the "Dunlop

65" golf ball was named for his second round). A 72 in the third round stretched the lead to 10 strokes, and Cotton could afford to stumble in with a 79 and still win by five. His second British Open championship came at Carnoustie in 1937 when he shot a final-round 71 in a driving rainstorm to beat a field that included the entire U.S. Ryder Cup team.

Cotton finished third in both 1936 and '38, then fourth in the first post–World War II Open in 1946. Turning 40 didn't slow him down. At Muirfield in 1948, he won his third Open, again on the strength of a great round, a second-round 66. He won by five strokes.

Though he played very little in the United States, Cotton was one of the first British pros to frequently compete on the European continent and he was a veteran of Ryder Cup play. Later, he became a noted teacher and writer on the game, eventually settling in Portugal.

Career Highlights

Achievements: Won 1934, 1937, and 1948 British Opens and placed among the top four six other times. Won 1946 and 1947 French Opens. Captured two PGA Matchplay titles and five other British events in the 1930s. Veteran of Ryder Cup Matches. Defeated Walter Hagen, 3 & 2, in a challenge match. Member of PGA/World Golf Hall of Fame.

Fred Couples

○ ○ ○

ONE OF THE MOST TALENTED players of his generation, Fred Couples is also one of the most laid-back personalities. One can only wonder what he might have achieved if he were more highly motivated or if back problems hadn't slowed him soon after he reached his prime. Still, Couples has compiled an impressive record in the 1980s and '90s and has been one of the game's most popular players.

Couples grew up in Seattle, then went to the University of Houston, where he was an All-American. He left school early to turn pro at age 21, and he hit the Tour in 1981 with a natural swing that produced long, left-to-right shots without his having to worry about swing mechanics. Couples won his first tournament in 1983 and captured the prestigious Players Championship the next year at age 24. Success may have come too quickly, however. Couples managed only one win in the next five campaigns, and he suffered a disappointing loss to Christy O'Connor Jr. in a crucial 1989 Ryder Cup Match.

That setback seemed to spur Couples on, however. By 1991, Couples was the leader of the U.S.

Ryder Cup team. He'd won once in 1990 and twice in 1991, when he was PGA Tour Player of the Year. In 1992, Couples was clearly the best player in the game. In one stretch he finished first twice and second twice in four straight tournaments; shortly thereafter, he won the Masters for his first major title.

Couples was uncomfortable in the spotlight, however, and recoiled from the attention his No. 1 status brought. Famously, he once said that he never answered the phone because he was afraid there would be someone on the other end. His "hot streak" then came to a halt.

Couples won only once in 1993, though he finished in the top 10 on the money list for the fourth straight year. Starting in 1994, Couples was hampered by back problems. He was forced to cut back his schedule, and, when he did play, he was often in pain. Still, he managed to win the 1996 Players Championship, bringing him up to 12 career victories.

CAREER HIGHLIGHTS

Earnings: $8,437,102
PGA Tour Victories: 12
Achievements: Won 1992 Masters; 1984 and 1996 Players Championships. Vardon Trophy winner and Tour Player of the Year in 1991 and 1992. Led Tour in earnings in 1992. Member of U.S. Ryder Cup teams in 1989, 1991, 1993, and 1995. Skins Game winner in 1995 and 1996.

Ben Crenshaw

○ ○ ○

He came out of the University of Texas in 1973 with a long swing, a silky putting stroke, and an amateur portfolio that stamped him as the game's next great star. Today, Ben Crenshaw's swing is considerably shorter, and he has compiled an outstanding record as a professional while falling a bit short of the lofty peaks predicted of him. One thing remains the same: his sweet putting stroke.

Indeed, Crenshaw will go down in history as one of the greatest putters in the game. Thus, it is perhaps no surprise that his two major titles have come in the Masters at Augusta National, where putting is paramount. In fact, in addition to winning the Masters in 1984 and '95, he has two seconds, two thirds, and two fourths there.

Crenshaw grew up in Austin, Texas, and stayed in town to play for the Longhorns, winning an unprecedented three consecutive NCAA Championships in 1971, '72, and '73 (sharing the second with teammate Tom Kite). He seemed ready to take the world by storm when, in the fall of 1973, he won his first event as a member of the PGA Tour, the San Antonio-Texas Open.

Crenshaw was plagued by wildness off the tee, however, and didn't post his next win until 1976. He claimed three victories that year and finished second on the money list; both would remain career highs. Though he has been plagued by inconsistency throughout his career, the popular Crenshaw had 19 victories through 1997 and had finished among the top 10 money winners seven times.

More than any other player, Crenshaw loves and respects the game's history, so the major championships are especially important to him. His first decade as a pro brought nothing but frustration—two seconds at the Masters, two seconds at the British Open, a playoff loss at the PGA Championship, and a third-place finish at the U.S. Open. Finally, he broke through at the 1984 Masters. Crenshaw's win at the 1995 Masters was also an emotional one, coming a week after the death of his longtime teacher, Harvey Penick.

CAREER HIGHLIGHTS

Earnings: $7,022,091
PGA Tour Victories: 19
Achievements: Won 1984 and 1995 Masters; 1983 Byron Nelson Classic; 1995 Grand Slam of Golf; 1971, 1972, and 1973 NCAA titles. Posted runner-up finishes in Masters, British Open, and PGA Championship. Four-time member of U.S. Ryder Cup team. Noted golf historian and course architect.

JOHN DALY

○ ○ ○

THE LEGEND OF LONG JOHN DALY began in 1991 at Crooked Stick Golf Club outside Indianapolis, where he made the PGA Championship field as seventh alternate and pummeled the course into submission. Daly was a 25-year-old rookie when he stole the headlines by winning that PGA by three strokes. He's stayed in the headlines ever since, though not always for flattering reasons.

Daly's stunning win made him an instant folk hero, partly for his long-hitting, all-out style of play ("grip it and rip it," he called it) and partly because he exuded an unpretentious, everyman appeal. It also made him instantly rich, thanks to endorsement contracts. But Daly was a flawed hero. He lived life to the hilt off the course as well as on. The year before he joined the PGA Tour, while he was on the Nike Tour, Daly nearly died after a drinking binge. Unfortunately, he didn't learn his lesson. A continuing alcohol problem led to erratic behavior, culminating at the end of 1993 when police were called to his home after Daly started smashing things.

That, in addition to several instances of withdrawing in the middle of a round, led to suspension from the PGA Tour and a first stint in alcohol rehabilitation in early 1994. A couple months after rejoining the Tour, he won the BellSouth Classic. In 1995, Daly captured his second major championship when he tamed the winds of St. Andrews to win the British Open in a playoff over Costantino Rocca. Daly also averaged 289 yards per drive during the 1995 season, then a Tour record.

Still, all was not well. Though Daly's British Open win again showed that he was capable of great things when his game was on, too often he succumbed to wild driving and an indifferent attitude. Daly finished no better than 10th in any tournament in 1996, but worse news was that he was back to drinking again. He left the Tour in the spring of 1997 for another attempt at alcohol rehab, with the jury still out on whether he would get his life in order and fulfill his potential of being one of the top players in the game. He returned later in the 1997 season and enjoyed a mild degree of success, but Daly cannot be considered a cinch to return to the top of his game. Time will tell.

CAREER HIGHLIGHTS
Earnings: $2,047,856
PGA Tour Victories: 4
Achievements: Won 1991 PGA Championship; 1995 British Open. Joined Jack Nicklaus, Tom Watson, and Johnny Miller as only Americans to win two majors before turning 30. Has finished third in Masters and Tour Championship. Averaged then-record 289 yards per drive in 1995.

BETH DANIEL

○ ○ ○

WHEN SHE JOINED THE LPGA TOUR in 1979, Beth Daniel had a tough act to follow: Nancy Lopez had won nine tournaments in a phenomenal rookie campaign the year before. Although Daniel did not match those numbers, she proved to be a worthy challenger, leading the LPGA money list in her second and third seasons on Tour on the way to an outstanding and lucrative career.

Daniel came to the LPGA Tour with excellent credentials. The South Carolina native won the U.S. Women's Amateur in 1975 at the age of 18, and she won it again in 1977. She was a member of the U.S. Curtis Cup team in 1976 and '78. While playing golf at Furman University, Daniel even spent some time playing for the men's team when she felt she wasn't getting enough competition with the women's team.

After winning one tournament and ranking 10th in earnings as a rookie, Daniel won five tournaments in 1980 and two in 1981, with victories in the World Championship of Women's Golf lifting her to the money title in both years. (Her $231,000 in 1980 made her the first LPGA player to crack the $200,000 mark.) She scored five more wins in 1982.

The rest of Daniel's career followed an up-and-down pattern, with slumps caused by injuries, illness, or just poor play, followed by bursts of excellence. After winning only once from 1984 to '88, Daniel won four times in the second half of 1989 and regained No. 1 status in 1990. That year, Daniel claimed seven victories, including her only career major at the LPGA Championship, and set an earnings record ($863,578) that would last for six years. Her 70.38 scoring average still stands as a record. Following a couple of mediocre years, Daniel bounced back in 1994.

The 5'10" Daniel is one of the LPGA's longest hitters and best ball-strikers. In addition to the three money titles, she has been named Player of the Year three times (1980, '90, '94) and won the Vare Trophy three times (1989, '90, '94) while racking up 32 career victories. In 1996, she became the third LPGA player to reach $5 million in career earnings, following Betsy King and Pat Bradley.

CAREER HIGHLIGHTS

Earnings: $4,972,216
LPGA Tour Victories: 32
Achievements: Won 1990 LPGA Championship; 1979 World Ladies; 1975 and 1977 U.S. Women's Amateurs. Tour Player of the Year in 1980, 1990, and 1994. Vare Trophy winner in 1989, 1990, and 1994. Led Tour in earnings in 1980, 1981, and 1990. Third player in LPGA history to earn $5 million.

JIMMY DEMARET

○ ○ ○

Some years after he had quit the competitive golf scene, Jimmy Demaret was asked if he would have won more had he taken golf more seriously. His response was typically candid. "If I had," he said, "I wouldn't have won anything."

In fact, James Newton Demaret, born in Houston in 1910, took his golf quite seriously. He won three Masters and 28 other tournaments on the PGA Tour, and by all accounts of his contemporaries was one of the best wind players the game has ever seen. With his enormous hands, and from a stance in which his feet were but a few inches apart, Demaret was a wizard at manipulating the golf ball. It's just that the times of golf gravity were interspersed, rather liberally, with times of frolic.

Indeed, it could be said that Demaret's vivacity and love of life gave as much to the game as did his wonderful talent. Perhaps more. Demaret, like most of his generation of golfers, got into the game as a caddie. When he joined the pro tour in 1927, all golfers wore the same style of clothing—brown or gray slacks, brown or black shoes, a white dress shirt, a tie, and sometimes a fedora hat. The clothing was not only conservative in color and cut, but the materials tended to be heavy and, in hot-weather locker rooms, "kind of stank," said Jimmy.

So one day in the late 1930s, while in New York City, Demaret visited a shop in the garment district where movie stars had their clothes made. There he saw bolts of lightweight materials in a kaleidoscope of bright colors. As Demaret remembered, he had acquired his taste for colors from his father, a house painter who, in the days before paints were mixed by machine, would mix by hand and test shades on the walls of his home. Jimmy asked if he could get some shirts and slacks made of such goods. Told the stuff was for ladies' garments, Jimmy said he didn't care, he wanted to play golf in them. A sartorial revolution in golf got under way. Not only did golfers begin to wear more lively looking clothing, but the clothes were lighter, and the shirts in particular made swinging a club easier.

It is difficult to measure precisely all other contributions to the game Demaret made in his long career, because many evolved from his sunny disposition. He had an infectious smile and an even more jolly laugh, told jokes with a relish, and had the gift of a professional entertainer. As a young man, he sang at a Texas nightclub owned by a man who was his first sponsor on the pro Tour. Golf quote books are peppered with Demaret witticisms. When one struggling golfer asked Demaret for advice, Jimmy shot back: "Take two weeks off—then quit the game."

> *"Colorful" doesn't begin to describe Demaret. He was labeled by one writer as "the affable eyesore of the professional golfing brigade."*

Actually, in the days before golf was televised, Demaret was often asked to do radio play-by-play broadcasts of golf tournaments. He infused them with his elfin, improvisational spirit, the most memorable call coming upon the second shot Lew Worsham holed from 105 yards to win the Tam O'Shanter World Championship in 1953. "The damn thing went in the hole," Demaret reported. When television did come to golf, Demaret was on the ground floor. For five years, he was a witty and incisive commentator (with Gene Sarazen) on the Emmy Award-winning television program *Shell's Wonderful World of Golf*. The show aired in the 1960s and had much to do with the growth of golf in the U.S. and around the rest of the world.

Demaret's association with the producer of the Shell show, Fred Raphael, led to the beginning of the Senior PGA Tour. Through Demaret's connections and influence, the made-for-TV competition Legends of Golf hit the air in 1978 with the team of Sam Snead and Gardner Dickinson prevailing. Bringing back to legitimate competition famous Tour pros in their 50s and beyond, the tournament was the stimulus—the "father"—of the Senior PGA Tour. The first 12 tournaments were played at Onion Creek C.C. in Austin, Texas, on the course Demaret designed.

But perhaps Demaret's finest contribution to the golfing landscape is The Champions Golf Club in Houston, which he originated and owned along with Jack Burke Jr. The two courses—Jackrabbit and Cypress Creek—are both superb layouts. The latter held a Ryder Cup Match (1967), a U.S. Open ('69), and a U.S. Amateur ('95). Although he had input, Demaret didn't design the courses. However, he did leave his unique imprint by making sure there were many colorful flowers trimming the grounds. Even more to the point, Demaret saw to the construction of a men's locker room that is the epitome of good fellowship—a warm and friendly place with a big and finely wooded bar, where golfers could spend many a sagacious hour talking the game and just having fun. A Demaret kind of place.

CAREER HIGHLIGHTS
Earnings: $173,982
PGA Tour Victories: 31
Achievements: Won 1940, 1947, and 1950 Masters. Vardon Trophy winner in 1947. Led 1947 Tour in earnings. Won seven Tour events in 1940. Competed in the Ryder Cup three times between 1947 and 1951, winning each time. Member of PGA/World Golf Hall of Fame. Influenced founding of Senior PGA Tour with his Legends of Golf TV competition in 1978.

Roberto De Vicenzo

○ ○ ○

Considering he is the greatest golfer ever from South America, it is unfortunate that Argentina's Roberto De Vicenzo is best remembered for his scorecard blunder that cost him a chance to win the 1968 Masters. The globetrotting De Vicenzo won somewhere in the neighborhood of 200 tournaments (perhaps as many as 230) around the world, including eight in sporadic appearances in the U.S.

The one that got away came in Augusta in 1968 on De Vicenzo's 45th birthday, when he shot a magnificent 65 in the final round to apparently tie Bob Goalby for first place. But fellow competitor Tommy Aaron had marked a 4 instead of a 3 for De Vicenzo on the 17th hole, and the Argentinean signed the incorrect scorecard. Once De Vicenzo signed the card, he was stuck with the 4 on the 17th for a total of 66 and a second-place finish. Three weeks later, he won the Houston Champions International.

De Vicenzo's history at the British Open came to a better end, though for a long time it seemed he was destined to be a perennial also-ran there. In his first three attempts—in 1948, '49, and '50—he finished third, second, and third. He went on to also place third in 1956, '60, and '64. Finally, in 1967, De Vicenzo won the event at Hoylake, finishing two strokes ahead of Jack Nicklaus, to become the oldest British Open champion of this century (44). For good measure, he added yet another third-place finish in 1969.

De Vicenzo started humbly as a caddie's assistant at a course near his home in Buenos Aires. He quickly showed a talent for the game, and at age 21 he won the Argentine Open and PGA. An international career soon followed. He was known as one of the game's best ball-strikers, though he was sometimes a shaky putter. De Vicenzo collected national open titles like they were trinkets; so many, in fact, that no one is quite sure of the exact number (perhaps as many as 39, in 14 different countries). Though he never won the U.S. Open, De Vicenzo did capture the first U.S. Senior Open, in 1980.

CAREER HIGHLIGHTS
Tour Victories: 8 (U.S.)
Achievements: Won 1967 British Open; 1980 U.S. Senior Open. Is believed to have won national open titles in 14 different countries and close to 200 tournaments worldwide. Finished second in 1968 Masters when he signed an incorrect scorecard that added one stroke. Posted seven top-three British Open finishes. Member of PGA/World Golf Hall of Fame.

LEO DIEGEL

○ ○ ○

A WINNER OF 30 PGA TOUR EVENTS in the 1920s and '30s, including the PGA Championship in 1928 and '29, Leo Diegel nonetheless is remembered for his close calls as much as for his victories. As talented as any of his contemporaries except, perhaps, Bobby Jones, Diegel was a nervous player and incessant worrier. The Michigan native could never capture the U.S. Open or British Open despite finishing among the top four on seven different occasions. "They keep trying to give me a championship, but I won't take it," he once said.

At the British Open, Diegel finished third in 1929 after leading going into the 36-hole final day, second in 1930, and second in 1933 when he missed a short putt on the final hole which would have put him in a playoff. At the U.S. Open, he lost the lead on the back nine and tied for second in 1920, was third in 1926 and '31, and fourth in 1932. In 1925, he could have won by playing the last six holes in even par; he played them 6-over instead.

Diegel's greatest moments came in the PGA Championship. On his way to winning the event in 1928 at Five Farms Country Club in Baltimore, Diegel ended Walter Hagen's streak of 22 straight match wins and four consecutive titles with a quarterfinal victory. It was an especially sweet win, since Diegel had blown a five-up lead in losing to Hagen in 40 holes in a 1926 quarterfinal and lost to the Haig in the 1927 final. In '28, Diegel demolished Gene Sarazen, 9 & 8, in the semifinals and beat Al Espinosa in the final. Diegel beat Sarazen and Hagen again in the 1929 PGA Championship before beating 1928 U.S. Open champion Johnny Farrell in the final. Diegel was also a terror in the Canadian Open, which he won in 1924, '25, '28, and '29.

Diegel's problems with nerves manifested themselves most strongly on the greens. He eventually came up with a solution, an unorthodox putting style where he bent way over and stuck both of his elbows out, a method that became known as "diegeling." For a while it was successful, but it too eventually failed him. Diegel was a member of every Ryder Cup team between 1927 and 1933.

CAREER HIGHLIGHTS
PGA Tour Victories: 30
Achievements: Won 1928 and 1929 PGA Championships; 1924, 1925, 1928, and 1929 Canadian Opens. Finished among the top eight in 11 U.S. or British Opens, including second-place showings in each. Won five Tour events in 1925. Member of four U.S. Ryder Cup teams between 1927 and 1933.

CHICK EVANS

○ ○ ○

THE LEGACY CHARLES "CHICK" EVANS left through his golf will continue to bear rich fruit for as long as the world remains civilized. It will far outdistance his achievements as a champion golfer, as superb as they were.

Evans was born in 1890 in Indianapolis. When he was three, the family moved to Chicago, and Evans was identified with the Windy City for the rest of his long life. He began in golf as a caddie at the Edgewater Golf Course on Chicago's north side, where in time he would become an honored member. Tall and slender, he soon developed a fine golf swing noted for its economy of movement, and by the age of 16 he was clearly marked for high achievement at the game.

In 1906, Evans qualified for the prestigious Western Amateur for the first time. He would take the title eight times, the first in 1909. In 1910, Evans reached another, higher level as a champion. He won the Western Open (in that era one of golf's major titles), defeating the best professionals in the game in doing so. No amateur would win this event again until 1985. In 1911, Evans won another highly regarded event, the North and South Amateur, and that year also added the French Amateur to his record.

In 1914, Evans came within inches of tying Walter Hagen at the U.S. Open when his pitch shot on the last hole just missed. In general, his annual quest for the national championships—the U.S. Open and Amateur—were invariably frustrating. A brilliant striker of the ball, especially with his irons, Evans was at best an erratic putter. In one event, before the club limitation rule was effected, he carried four putters in his bag. An extrovert with a bright smile, Evans liked being the center of attention. But for some reason he was hampered in his earlier days by a certain nervousness in the nationals. No less a figure than Harry Vardon once said Evans was the best amateur he had ever played with in the United States, yet the sandy-haired, freckle-faced Chicagoan could not get past the semifinals of the U.S. Amateur.

Evans, who struggled mightily with his putter, became so discouraged at one point that he carried four of them in his bag.

Finally, in 1916, the "uncrowned amateur champion" broke through. In June of that year, Evans won the U.S. Open at the Minikahda Golf Course in Minneapolis with a record-setting score of 286, 2-under-par, that would hold up for the next 20 years. In September, at age 26, he defeated defending champion Bob Gardner in the final of the U.S. Amateur, at the Merion Cricket Club outside Philadelphia, to become the first player to win both national titles in one year. He would win the Amateur again in 1920, when he survived a 41-hole marathon in round three before trouncing the legendary Francis Ouimet in the finals.

With World War I underway in Europe, Evans used his celebrity in 1917 and 1918 to help raise funds for the Red Cross. To that end, he traveled some 26,000 miles to 41 cities playing exhibitions. But his social consciousness and sense of responsibility reached their highest point beginning in 1930, when the Great Depression was beginning to take hold of the nation. Evans's fame had brought him many offers to endorse products and earn appearance money. Dedicated to amateurism (he quit caddying before his 16th birthday to preserve his amateur status, as the Amateur Code demanded in those days), he turned all money offers down. However, he was allowed to use monies received from the sale of his golf instructional phonograph records for the establishment of a caddie scholarship fund instituted in his name. Evans Scholarships were meant for young male (and later female) caddies who could not afford a college education but qualified for one with good grades in high school.

The first two Evans Scholarship recipients entered Northwestern University in 1930, and since that time the program has accounted for more than 5,000 college and university graduates from over 30 different schools around the country.

The program has long been administered by the Western Golf Association, which raises the funds (over $5 million a year) through individual contributions and the Western Open. Many Evans Scholars have gone farther in life than they might have otherwise, because the thoughtful Evans never forgot his own rather humble beginnings and an appreciation of learning he inherited from his mother.

Evans formally retired from national competition in 1939. However, in 1962 he made an honorary 50th appearance in the U.S. Amateur, and he continued to compete in local Chicago tournaments. In the latter, he would appear with a thin golf bag over his shoulder containing 10 clubs (a number he advocated as enough, on the notion that more people would then be able to afford to play golf), all of them extra long. In this, he was some 20 years ahead of the vogue for longer-than-standard clubs.

CAREER HIGHLIGHTS

Achievements: Won 1916 U.S. Open; 1916 and 1920 U.S. Amateur. Won Western Amateur eight times beginning in 1909. Using only seven clubs, set U.S. Open record that lasted 20 years with 286 total in 1916. Became first man to win U.S. Open and U.S. Amateur in the same year. Member of PGA/World Golf Hall of Fame. Developed Evans Scholarships for golf caddies to attend college.

NICK FALDO

○ ○ ○

ONE DAY IN 1990, Nick Faldo asked Ben Hogan how to win the U.S. Open. Hogan replied, "Shoot the lowest score." Faldo thought the man was having a joke. He asked the question again. And got the same reply. End of conversation.

Faldo didn't really need to ask. His game was in the Hogan mold, a paragon of consistency derived from solid and well-understood swing fundamentals combined with unassailable concentration as well as an unquenchable thirst for practice. The very swing Faldo developed and which brought him to the apex of the game has a certain Hogan-esque quality: compact, controlled, and consistent.

If his parents had anything to do about it, Nicholas Alexander Faldo, born in 1957 in Hertfordshire, England, was going to be something special. His mother in particular had various visions of what her only child would become—an actor, a dancer, a clothing model, a concert pianist. She never had golf in mind, but that was the direction her strong-willed son chose. However, the training of the boy's mind to be very good at whatever he decided to do certainly took.

At age 14, after watching Jack Nicklaus play golf on television, Faldo resolved he would give the game a go. A fine natural athlete—tall, well-built, and strong—he got the knack for the game quickly. He became a regular contender in British junior amateur golf, and in 1975 he won the British Youths and English Amateur championships. That led to a golf scholarship at the University of Houston, a perennial collegiate golf power. But after only 10 weeks on campus, Faldo decided that was not the way to advance his career, and he was in a hurry. He dropped out, returned home, and in late 1976 turned pro. He was 19 years old.

Faldo had some success early on playing the European PGA Tour, winning 11 tournaments from 1977 to 1984, plus one on the U.S. PGA Tour. However, he discerned that if he was going to go to the very top, he would have to make some major changes in his swing. Working closely with South African teaching professional David Leadbetter, Faldo completely revamped his technique. It took a full two years to bring the changes up to speed. In 1985 and '86, he won nothing in either Europe or the U.S., where he played periodically. Then, everything he had been working on fell into place. In 1987, Faldo won the British Open, making 18 pars in the final round to catch and pass a faltering Paul Azinger.

Faldo's star had now completely cleared the horizon, and his accomplishments began to multiply. In 1988, he won twice in Europe and lost in a playoff with Curtis Strange for the U.S. Open. In 1989, he captured his second major title, the

Faldo started out as a golf prodigy. At age 15, on the first hole he ever played, he hit a driver and then a 3-wood onto the green of a 450-yard par 4.

Masters, after a playoff with Scott Hoch. He won four other events that year on the European Tour. In 1990, Faldo again won the Masters, again in a playoff (with Raymond Floyd), to become only the second successful defender of that much-prized title. That same year, he tied for third in the U.S. Open and won his second British Open crown. He won his national championship a third time in 1992.

For all his great success over a 10-year stretch, Faldo became dissatisfied with his game. There were uncharacteristic lapses in his concentration and his shot-making. They may well have been related to the breakup of his marriage, from which three children were born and which was treated by the scandal-mongering element of the British press with particularly disgusting venom.

In any case, Faldo went back to the drawing board for swing and playing adjustments and decided to play full-time on the U.S. PGA Tour, which he felt was the most competitive in the world. The decision paid dividends almost immediately. In 1995, he won the Doral-Ryder Open, a mini-major in that it is played on a difficult course and always has one of the strongest competitive fields. Then, in 1996, he won his third Masters.

A self-possessed man with an acerbic wit that put off the golf press, yellow and otherwise, Faldo's success has often been questioned. In making 18 pars to win his first British Open, some speculated he didn't want to win so much as to simply let others falter and hand him the prize. He won his first Masters when Hoch missed very short putts, his second when Floyd unaccountably pulled a 7-iron approach shot into the water beside the 11th green. In his third Masters victory, Greg Norman handed it over by shooting a final-round 78.

In making 18 straight pars, it wasn't as if he didn't try to make a birdie or two. No putts dropped. Against Hoch, he fired a final-round 65 at Augusta National and won in sudden-death with a birdie. Against Floyd, Faldo had a last-round 67 to Floyd's 72. Against Norman, Faldo had a brilliant final-round 69. How then might Faldo answer his detractors? He won because he shot the lowest scores.

Career Highlights

Earnings: $2,919,818
PGA Tour Victories: 6
Achievements: Won 1989, 1990, and 1996 Masters; 1987, 1990, and 1992 British Opens. Winner of 33 international events as a professional. First international player to win PGA Tour Player of the Year Award in 1990. Led Sony World Ranking for record 81 weeks in 1993–94. Led European Tour Order of Merit (earnings) in 1983 and 1992. Has been a European Ryder Cup team regular since 1977.

JOHNNY FARRELL

○ ○ ○

WHILE AMATEUR BOBBY JONES and flamboyant Walter Hagen were dominating the major championships in the late 1920s, Johnny Farrell quietly went about the business of winning as many tournaments as he could on the developing pro Tour. He finished with 30 professional wins, 22 of which are now considered official victories. Farrell's finest hour came in the 1928 U.S. Open, where he defeated Jones in a 36-hole playoff to claim his only major title.

Farrell, born in White Plains, New York, in 1901, caddied as a youngster. By age 21, he was a good enough player to score his first professional win, the Shawnee Open. Not a long hitter, Farrell nevertheless owned an extremely graceful swing and became known as a fine putter and accurate player. He was also considered one of the best dressers of his day.

Farrell hit his stride in 1926 and won a total of 18 tournaments from 1926 to '28. In the 1928 U.S. Open at Olympia Fields, Farrell made up five shots on Jones with a final-round 72 to force a playoff. He then won the next day, 143–144, sinking a seven-foot putt on the final hole.

The victory made up for the disappointment of the 1925 U.S. Open, where Farrell wound up in third place after a final-round 78. He also was third in 1926, fifth in 1923, seventh in 1927, eighth in 1930, ninth in 1933, and 10th in 1931. Farrell also had a consistent record in the PGA Championship, though he never won it. The closest he came was in 1929, when he lost to Leo Diegel in the final, 6 & 4. He reached the semifinals in 1926, losing to Hagen, and again in 1933, losing to Gene Sarazen, and got to the quarterfinals three more times. Farrell finished second in the 1929 British Open, six strokes behind Hagen, and he played on the first three U.S. Ryder Cup teams (1927, '29, and '31).

Farrell won money in every start in 1923 and '24 before breaking through as a regular. His winning days came to an end in 1931, except for a win every now and then in a couple of minor events. He went on to become the long-time professional at Baltusrol in New Jersey.

CAREER HIGHLIGHTS
PGA Tour Victories: 22
Achievements: Won 1928 U.S. Open in 36-hole playoff over Bobby Jones, 143–144. Finished second in 1929 British Open. Captured seven Tour events in 1927 and five in 1926. Earned money in every start during 1923 and 1924. Member of three U.S. Ryder Cup teams.

JIM FERRIER

○ ○ ○

ONE OF THE FIRST in a growing line of world-class golfers to come from Australia, Jim Ferrier emigrated to the United States in 1940 at the age of 25 and finished his PGA Tour career with 18 victories and one major title, the 1947 PGA Championship.

Ferrier worked as a sportswriter in his younger days while tearing up the amateur circuit in Australia. He won the Australian Amateur four times between 1935 and '39, and he also captured the Australian Open in 1938 and '39. He made a trip to Great Britain in 1936 and finished second in the British Amateur. Having done all he could in his native land, Ferrier decided to come to America. He entered the 1940 U.S. Open as an amateur, but a question arose as to his amateur status because he had written an instruction book, and he turned professional later in the year. His professional career started much more slowly than his amateur successes, for he went at least three years without a victory.

Ferrier scored his first pro win in 1944, but that was all he owned coming into the 1947 PGA Championship. Ferrier reached the final at Plum Hollow in Detroit against local favorite Chick Harbert. Concerned that overzealous spectators would kick his ball into trouble, or Harbert's ball out of it, Ferrier hired two policemen to walk each side of the fairway as he played. The Australian scored a 2 & 1 victory, calling it "the best $100 I ever spent."

Though he was a burly 6'4", Ferrier's putting and short game were his strong suits. He had an unorthodox swing, with a dipping motion attributed to a knee injury suffered in his youth. Ferrier was at his best at the start of the 1950s. He finished second on the money list in 1950 and rang up five victories in 1951, including three wins in a row. He never managed to win a second major, just barely missing his best chance at the 1950 Masters. Needing a 38 on Augusta's back nine to win, Ferrier shot a 41 instead and finished second to Jimmy Demaret. Ferrier came in third in the 1952 Masters, and, though he was by then well past his prime, was runner-up in the 1960 PGA Championship at stroke play, finishing one shot behind Jay Hebert.

CAREER HIGHLIGHTS

Earnings: $183,798
PGA Tour Victories: 18
Achievements: Won 1947 PGA Championship; 1950 and 1951 Canadian Opens; 1938 and 1939 Australian Opens. Finished second in 1950 Masters. Was second in Tour earnings in 1950. Won five Tour events in 1951, including three in a row. Captured four Australian Amateur titles in 1930s.

RAYMOND FLOYD

◦ ◦ ◦

RAYMOND FLOYD'S FATHER was a career Army man, and his son's march on the golf course mirrors his being raised on military bases—back absolutely straight and head high at attention, like a good soldier.

Raymond's carriage may have had something to do with the golf swing he developed. Tall but with rather short arms and a heavily muscled upper body, Floyd created a peculiar-looking swing. It has been likened to the construct of a football linebacker, or perhaps a windmill with a screw or two loose. The club goes back rather sharply to the inside with a dip of his left shoulder, then is raised seemingly straight up to the completion of the backswing. The zigzag route is pretty much repeated going back to impact.

Had he not stood so tall at address, the swing might have been more fluid and formful. Floyd's response to outsiders' comments about his swing has always been, with a sly smile, "It ain't how; it's how many." Exactly. And if he'd tried to shape a golf swing in the "classic" mode, he might well have taken too many. In a game where less is more, Raymond Floyd got well onto the lesser side of the ledger, and he has stayed there far longer than the pattern of his golf swing would suggest possible.

Clearly, Floyd simply has a gift for the essence of the game, keeping the ball in play and finding a way to make a score. Floyd was an excellent baseball pitcher early on—his performance in his high school days was so impressive that he was offered a $30,000 bonus to sign with a major-league club. He instead opted for golf, a game he was inspired to play by his father and for which he also had obvious potential. And yet, early on, he almost threw his gift to the winds.

The game was easy for me as a kid, and I had to play a while to find out how hard it is."
—RAYMOND FLOYD

One golf observer once said it was a wonder Floyd made it in golf when his first "heroes" were Doug Sanders and Al Besselink, two older fellows and outstanding golfers who had a penchant for wine, women, and song. Floyd would later recount that his first 12 years as a touring pro (he began on the PGA circuit in 1963) were "just a means to an end," a way to make enough money to enable him to have fun elsewhere. He was also a notorious high-stakes gambler on his golf game. The consensus of the golf community in the early 1970s was that Floyd's talent was going to waste, even though he had won a PGA Championship (1969) and four other Tour events, and would never bear full fruit.

Then he met his wife, Maria, a strong personality in her own right who had a more conventional set of values. Everything was turned around. Raymond Floyd would become such an esteemed figure in the world of golf that he would become known simply as Raymond. Everyone knew who was meant. In 1975, having gone four years without a single victory and with the first of his three children just born, Floyd won the Kemper Open. He followed that up in 1976 with an astounding eight-shot victory in the Masters as well as a win in the World Open. From 1977 through 1992, he claimed victory 15 times, including another Masters, another PGA Championship, and the U.S. Open in 1986, which gave him the distinction of being, at 44, the oldest-ever winner of the national championship.

Floyd had a knack for winning the big ones, the tournaments with the best fields playing on the toughest courses. Along with his major victories, Floyd won the 1981 Tournament Players Championship, the 1982 Memorial, and the Doral-Ryder Open three times. The last Doral victory, in 1992, came just eight months before his 50th birthday, and it prepared him well for his entry to the Senior PGA Tour.

Floyd was expected to be a terror on the Senior circuit, and he definitely made that calculation a sound one. Right out of the box, late in 1992, he won three times, including the Senior Tour Championship, a senior major. He won twice in 1993 and four times in '94, including another Senior Tour Championship. In all, through 1995, Floyd had won 34 times on both the PGA and Senior PGA Tours. And just to show the young bucks of the next generation that he still could keep up, he entered 14 events on the PGA Tour from 1993 to '95 and finished in the top 10 three times—and nine times in the top 25.

Floyd, who won the 1983 Vardon Trophy for low stroke average (70.61), played on eight Ryder Cup teams and was nonplaying captain of another. Floyd is also one of just two golfers to win tournaments on the PGA Tour in four different decades. The other? Sam Snead.

CAREER HIGHLIGHTS

Earnings: $5,261,844 (PGA); $5,580,271 (SR)
Tour Victories: 22 (PGA); 13 (SR)
Achievements: Won 1986 U.S. Open; 1976 Masters; 1969 and 1982 PGA Championships; 1995 PGA Seniors Championship; 1994 Tradition; 1996 Senior Players Championship; 1992 and 1994 Senior Tour Championships. First player to win on PGA and Senior Tour in same year (1992). Vardon Trophy winner in 1993. Ryder Cup veteran, captaining U.S. team in 1989. Member of PGA/World Golf Hall of Fame.

DOUG FORD

◎ ◎ ◎

ONE OF THE MOST CONSISTENT PLAYERS of the 1950s, Doug Ford was known for two things—being the fastest player in golf and owning an excellent short game. Ford scored 19 victories on the PGA Tour between 1952 and 1963, including the 1955 PGA Championship and 1957 Masters.

Born in West Haven, Connecticut, Ford didn't join the Tour until 1950, when he was 27 years old. He finished in the top 20 money winners in each of his first 12 years on the circuit, and most of the time was in the top 10 (including every year from 1951 to 1960). He finished second in earnings in 1953 and 1957 and third in 1955. Ford was neither a classic striker of the ball nor a long hitter, but he was a feisty competitor and was deadly around the greens.

Ford was named PGA Player of the Year in 1955. He won the PGA Championship that year in his first appearance in the event (players were then required to complete an apprenticeship before becoming eligible), dominating from start to finish. After winning the qualifying medal, Ford won one of his matches 12 & 10 in rolling to the final against Cary Middlecoff. There, Ford birdied the 29th, 30th, and 32nd holes to go 3-up on the way to a 4 & 3 victory at Meadowbrook Country Club in Detroit.

Ford claimed another major at the 1957 Masters, coming from three strokes behind to win by three over Sam Snead with a closing 66, which at the time was the best final round in Masters history. He holed a bunker shot at the last hole at Augusta to put an exclamation point on the victory. The next year, he tied for second, one stroke behind Arnold Palmer. In 1997, he tied Sam Snead's record by making his 44th appearance in the Masters.

Ford won the Canadian Open twice, including his final career victory in 1963. His best finishes in the U.S. Open were a fifth in 1959 and a sixth in 1961. After the PGA Championship went to stroke play in 1958, Ford finished in the top 11 for five straight years, finishing fifth in 1961 and '62. He played for all four Ryder Cup teams between 1955 and 1961.

CAREER HIGHLIGHTS
Earnings: $414,663
PGA Tour Victories: 19
Achievements: Won 1955 PGA Championship; 1957 Masters; 1959 and 1963 Canadian Opens. Tour Player of the Year in 1955. Finished second in Tour earnings in 1953 and 1957 and third in 1955. Member of U.S. Ryder Cup teams four times between 1955 and 1961.

HUBERT GREEN

○ ○ ○

ALTHOUGH HE WAS FAR from the classic golfer, Hubert Green was a force to be reckoned with on the PGA Tour in the 1970s. Green's style was unorthodox on all types of shots. On full shots, he held his hands low and picked the club up quickly to the outside. On chip shots, he played the ball well back in his stance and held his hands forward. On putts, he bent well over and used a split-handed grip. It all worked well enough for Green to win 17 times during the '70s and 19 times in all, including the 1977 U.S. Open and 1985 PGA Championship.

Green, an Alabama native, won the Southern Amateur in 1966 and 1969. Following a brief stint as an assistant pro at Merion outside Philadelphia, he made his debut on the PGA Tour in 1971 and within four months claimed his first victory at the Houston Champions International. From 1973 through 1979, Green ranked no worse than 13th on the money list, with a best of third in 1974 when he won four times. In the spring of 1976, he won three straight tournaments—the Doral Eastern Open, Jacksonville Open, and Sea Pines Heritage Classic.

Green showed his true grit in winning the 1977 U.S. Open. He faced the pressure of being tied for the lead after one round, then ahead by one after rounds two and three. On Sunday afternoon, with four holes remaining, he was informed of a telephoned death threat. He elected to continue play and finished with a 70 to win by one stroke. Green finished in the top 10 in all but one Masters from 1974 to '80, but he never earned a green jacket. He came closest in 1978, when he led after three rounds and missed a three-foot birdie putt on the final green which would have tied him with Gary Player. Green was a three-time U.S. Ryder Cup player between the years 1977 and 1985.

Green's game began to deteriorate after 1979, but one of his two victories after that year came in a major, when he outlasted Lee Trevino at Cherry Hills in the 1985 PGA Championship. He joined the Senior PGA Tour in 1996 and immediately became a contender.

CAREER HIGHLIGHTS
Earnings: $2,588,884 (PGA); (SR) $556,402
PGA Tour Victories: 19
Achievements: Won 1977 U.S. Open; 1985 PGA Championship. Winner of four events twice, including Southern Open and Heritage Classic. Claimed three consecutive events in 1976. PGA Rookie of the Year in 1971. Member of U.S. Ryder Cup team in 1977, 1979, and 1985.

Ralph Guldahl

○ ○ ○

His up-and-down career may be one of the great mysteries of golf, but for a few years in the late 1930s Ralph Guldahl was the most dominant player in the game. The 6′3″ Texan is one of only six players ever to win back-to-back U.S. Opens, claiming the title in 1937 and again in '38. He was second in the Masters both of those years, winning it in 1939. And he won the Western Open, then one of the game's big events, in 1936, '37, and '38. Then his game suddenly vanished—for the second time.

Guldahl first emerged in 1932, when he won the Arizona Open at the age of 20. He nearly won the 1933 U.S. Open, missing a four-foot putt on the 72nd hole to finish one stroke behind Johnny Goodman. Then he went into a slump and quit the Tour in frustration in 1935. After changing his grip and spending long hours practicing his swing, Guldahl returned in 1936 and led the Tour in scoring average.

Guldahl beat Sam Snead by two strokes at Oakland Hills in 1937 to take his first U.S. Open title. He eagled the 8th hole and birdied the 9th, then learned he could beat Snead with a 37 on the back. "If I can't play this last nine in 37 strokes," he said, "I'm a bum and don't deserve to win the Open." Guldahl shot a 36 on the back to finish with a 69 and set a new U.S. Open 72-hole record of 281. The next year, at Cherry Hills, Guldahl also closed with a 69 to win by six strokes. At the Masters in 1939, Guldahl beat out Snead by one stroke with another final-round 69 and solidified his status as a force among golf's best players. Such status, however, was fleeting.

Guldahl won a couple tournaments in 1940, but the next year he struggled greatly. He took motion pictures of his swing and compared them with his swing when he won the Masters, but he couldn't find the fatal flaw. All he knew was that the winning touch had vanished. His enthusiasm for the game gone in a relatively brief period of time, Guldahl left the Tour in 1942 and, except for brief periods, never returned. No one can fully understand his highs or lows in the game.

Career Highlights

Earnings: approx. $50,000
PGA Tour Victories: 16
Achievements: Won 1937 and 1938 U.S. Opens; 1939 Masters; 1936, 1937, and 1938 Western Opens. Posted runner-up Masters finishes in 1937 and 1938. Led Tour in scoring average and won three tournaments in 1936. Member of PGA/World Golf Hall of Fame.

WALTER HAGEN

○ ○ ○

WALTER HAGEN WAS EFFECTIVELY the first American professional golfer—not golf professional, but professional golfer. He made his living only by playing the game. When Hagen did take his one and only head-pro job at a club, at the Oakland Hills Country Club outside Detroit, it was while the course was under construction. When it opened for play, he quit the post. It was not for Walter Hagen to stand for hours in the sun giving golf lessons; to spend his time in a small, cluttered shop selling clubs, balls, and tees; to be an underling in the employ of anyone. That was a brave way to go in the first decades of the 20th century, when golf was still new to the United States and there was only the merest beginnings of a tournament circuit.

Did Hagen foresee a time when many men might follow his lead? Probably not. Hagen was simply dancing to his own inner music. Still, in his daring Hagen had set a precedent. It was not to be followed by too many in his time, but he initiated the notion that an outstanding golfer could make his way in the world by showing off his talent to the public eye. As Herb Graffis, a pioneer golf periodical publisher, put it in 1980: "Today's [Tour] pros should light a candle every day of their lives in the memory of Walter Hagen." And because Hagen was such a colorful personality, he also got the game of golf on its way as a significant sporting pastime among the populace at large at a time when the game was played by a relative few.

How did Hagen do it? It wasn't with his long game. With his long, loose swing, he was often wild off the tee and inconsistently accurate even from the fairways. Nevertheless, Walter played at the highest level from 1914 to '36. During that 22-year period, Hagen won a total of 44 events, including two U.S. Opens, four British Opens, and a record-setting five PGA Championships, four of them in a row (1924–27). He did it with a vivid imagination when in trouble—an eye for finding a gap in the trees and a gift for fitting a ball through it—plus a magnificently deft touch as a chipper and putter. Just as important, he had not a doubt at all of his ability. Playing one of the most frustrating of games, he never let golf get him down. His "philosophy" of golf was expressed in a couple of simple homilies: If you find yourself hooking the ball on a given day, just aim to the right a little more; also, he expected to miss seven shots per round and didn't fret when they occurred. It was a philosophy that served him well.

While the majority of Hagen's victories were at stroke play, his forte was as a match-play competitor. In this mano-a-mano format, he was a master psychologist who, for one thing, knew full well that his disorderly tee-to-green game made him seem like easy pickings for the purer ball-strikers, but who would be rendered limp, if not angry, by Hagen's amazing recoveries from trouble on the course. Adding to that was the brio with which he pulled off his miracles. He also understood the effect of pressure on athletes. In this regard, Hagen's most memorable remark came when he was told, while preparing to spend a night on the town on the eve of the final match for the 1926 PGA Championship, that his opponent, the nervous Leo Diegel, was already in bed: "Yes," said Hagen, "but he isn't sleeping."

Walter Hagen reflected a classic American success story, the athlete playing his way out of humble circumstances. He was born in 1892 in Rochester, New York, the son of working-class German immigrants. His father, a blacksmith, advised his son to learn a trade and thought the boy a "bullhead" for passing up carpentry. As a youth, Hagen was an excellent ice skater and baseball player. His first athletic sights were set on playing major-league baseball, and in a tryout with the Philadelphia Phillies in the winter of 1912, he received a very favorable review. But he also had been playing golf, beginning as a preteen caddie. During the summer after his baseball tryout, he tied for fourth in the second golf tournament he had ever entered, the

U.S. Open. When he won that championship the next year, his future was settled.

What set Hagen apart, aside from his athletic gifts, was his instinct and flair for showmanship. "Barnum and Bailey rolled into one," said Graffis. But Hagen somehow gave his "circus act" a kind of salon quality. He had a way of walking with his head tilted up, like royalty, that—along with the lifestyle he developed—would earn him the lifelong sobriquet "Sir Walter."

Whether battling in a professional tournament or playing in a casual foursome, Hagen enjoyed himself. "You're only here for a short visit," he once said. "Don't hurry. Don't worry. And be sure to smell the flowers along the way."

His son, Walter Jr., once suggested that his dad's love of the high life came from the days when his father caddied at the Country Club of Rochester for such people as George Eastman (founder of Eastman Kodak) and other wealthy, sophisticated people. Hagen was beguiled by the talk he heard of travel and the high life. Watching from a respectable distance as the club members danced away summer evenings, the young Hagen was entranced. He did not resent the rich; he simply wanted a piece of their action. In Walter Jr.'s words: "It set Dad's standards. He always wanted a look of success." Walter Sr. put it another way, memorably: "I don't want to be a millionaire; I just want to live like one." He did just that, thanks to his remarkable skills.

And yet, for all the silk shirts, tailored knickers, jeweled cuff links, and other accoutrements associated with the high life that Hagen fancied, he also projected the down-to-earthiness of the common man. Certainly the ordinary citizen golfer could identify with Hagen's unkempt, razzmatazz golf. He stood at the ball with the wide stance of a home run hitter, made a rainbow-arc swing that ended with an unfettered lunge, sprayed shots all over the lot, and was consistently flirting with danger—from which he recovered with insouciant aplomb. Furthermore, with Hagen there was none of the dour gravity brought to the game by the Scottish pros who emigrated to the United States and were golf's first showcase players in the country. Hagen was a joy to watch because he obviously enjoyed what he was doing. He never complained about a golf course—he called them all "sporty little layouts"—and as a friend once remarked, he "never had a temper."

It was an intriguing combination Hagen put together, and through it he was a major factor in the growth of American golf. In the period when he was most active as a golfer, the pro Tour was in its embryonic state and paid little in purse money. Hagen earned most of his money playing exhibitions, some 4,000 18-hole outings from 1914 to 1941 that brought in an estimated $1 million. This was an impressive sum for the time, but what made it all the more so was that Hagen did not perform for preset fees and expenses. He barnstormed, playing to whatever size audience he could draw, usually at a dollar a ticket. And Sir Walter did not restrict himself to playing in established golf country. He also traveled to the hinterlands—the Dakotas, Wyoming—where the courses were usually quite primitive and where he had to pull in every golf fan and curiosity seeker within a 500-mile radius.

Hagen satisfied one and all, and he never slowed down the proceedings with dry dissertations on the mysteries of the game. He was the Johnny Appleseed of American golf. No one can say for certain how many persons Sir Walter inspired to take up golf, but a fair guess is that he corralled one for every dollar he made on the exhibition circuit alone, not counting their sons and daughters.

CAREER HIGHLIGHTS

PGA Tour Victories: 44
Achievements: Won 1914 and 1919 U.S. Opens; 1922, 1924, 1928, and 1929 British Opens; 1921, 1924, 1925, 1926, and 1927 PGA Championships. Defeated Bobby Jones in a special 72-hole match 11 & 10 in 1926. Led Tour five times in tournaments won. Member of PGA/World Golf Hall of Fame. Captained the U.S. team in the first six Ryder Cup Matches. Won an estimated $1 million playing in some 4,000 exhibition matches from 1914 to 1941.

SANDRA HAYNIE

○ ○ ○

THOUGH OVERSHADOWED by the great Kathy Whitworth, Sandra Haynie was one of the best and most consistent players in the women's game from 1961 to '75. Haynie enjoyed her biggest moments in the sun in 1974, when she won the U.S. Women's Open and LPGA Championship. She is one of only three players to sweep those events in a single year (along with Mickey Wright, 1961, and Meg Mallon, 1991).

Haynie was born in Fort Worth, Texas, and made a fast start in the game by winning the Texas Amateur in 1958 (at age 15) and '59. She turned pro in 1961 and claimed her first victory in 1962 at age 18. Haynie won at least one tournament every year for 14 years starting in 1962, claiming 39 titles in that span. She finished in the top five on the money list 11 times and was second five times, most recently in 1982. Though Haynie never earned the money title, she took Player of the Year honors in 1970.

Her best year, however, was 1974, when she captured a career-high six victories, including the only two major championships then contested. First, she beat JoAnne Carner by two strokes to win her second LPGA Championship (the first came in 1965). Then, at La Grange Country Club outside Chicago, Haynie pulled off one of the most dramatic finishes in U.S. Women's Open history. She birdied the last two holes to win by one stroke over Carol Mann and Beth Stone, sinking a 75-foot putt on the 17th and a 15-footer on the 18th for a 295 total.

Slowed by arthritis and knee surgery, Haynie retired twice and successfully came back each time. After sitting out most of 1977–80, she won three events in 1981 and 1982, finishing second on the money list the latter year. Sidelined again from 1985 to '87, Haynie returned for 1988 and '89 to surpass $1 million in career earnings before calling it quits for good. Haynie finished with a total of 42 victories, tied with Carner for seventh-best all time. The Texan was known primarily as a very straight driver and steady player, hitting fairways and greens with regularity. She now heads a celebrity pro-am called "Swing Against Arthritis."

CAREER HIGHLIGHTS
Earnings: $1,055,875
LPGA Tour Victories: 42
Achievements: Won 1965 and 1974 LPGA Championships; 1974 U.S. Women's Open; 1982 Peter Jackson Classic. Followed Mickey Wright as second to win LPGA Championship and U.S. Women's Open in same year. Five-time runner-up in Tour earnings. Member of LPGA Hall of Fame.

HAROLD HILTON

○   ○   ○

ENGLISH AMATEUR HAROLD HILTON, whose career of winning major championships spanned the years 1892–1913, holds several significant distinctions. He is the only British player ever to win the U.S. Amateur, one of three amateurs to win the British Open (along with John Ball and Bobby Jones), and one of four to take the U.S. and British Amateurs in the same year (along with Jones, Lawson Little, and Bob Dickson). Many well-known professionals did not have the skills of the diminutive Hilton.

Hilton's earliest triumphs came in the British Open. At age 23, he won the 1892 Open at Muirfield, the first time the tournament was played at 72 holes. Five years later, Hilton captured the Open at his home course, Royal Liverpool. Trailing James Braid by three strokes after 54 holes, Hilton posted a closing 75 for a total of 314 and retreated to the clubhouse to play billiards while Braid tried to beat his score. Hilton emerged to watch Braid make a 4 at the last hole when he needed a 3 to tie. Late in his career, Hilton nearly added a third Open title. Also, he was one stroke out of a playoff at Royal St. George's in 1911, a year in which he would meet great success elsewhere.

Hilton was developing a reputation as better at stroke play than match play, having lost in the final of the British Amateur in 1891, '92, and '96. But he went on to win by an 8 & 7 margin in the 1900 final over James Robb and reclaimed the title in 1901. After a dry spell, he took his third and fourth British Amateurs in 1911 and 1913.

In 1911, at age 42, Hilton decided to make the overseas trip to America to try to win the U.S. Amateur. His appearance attracted much attention in the American press, and Hilton rolled to the final against Fred Herreshoff. The Englishman lost a 6-up lead before winning with a par on the 37th hole.

Hilton stood just 5'6". He took such a fast and furious swing that he often came up on his toes at impact and lost his hat at the finish. Nevertheless, he was a very accurate player. He also became editor of two publications, *Golf Monthly* and *Golf Illustrated*.

CAREER HIGHLIGHTS
Achievements: Won 1892 and 1897 British Opens; 1900, 1901, 1911, and 1913 British Amateurs; 1911 U.S. Amateur. Only British player ever to win U.S. Amateur and one of just three amateurs ever to win British Open. Designed several courses, wrote golf manuals, and edited two golf publications. Member of PGA/World Golf Hall of Fame.

BEN HOGAN

○ ○ ○

Ben Hogan's career in golf was a saga of overcoming, one that is legendary in its proportions. He grew up in difficult financial circumstances, and more significantly had to live with the calamity of his father's suicide. It took him years to overcome a basic swing flaw. Once he found the solution, he lost more time serving in the armed forces. Then, Hogan barely survived a devastating highway accident from which he suffered physical pain the rest of his life. But Hogan persevered to become one of golf's all-time great champions, not to mention one of the game's most intriguing personalities.

William Ben Hogan was born in 1912 in Stephenville, Texas, and was raised in nearby Dublin until the age of 10, when his father, Chester, took his own life. Following that tragic event, Ben's mother moved the family (Ben and his older sister and brother) to Fort Worth, where Ben, at age 12, learned of golf as a caddie and found his lifework.

As a teenager, Hogan clearly had enough innate ability to consider a future as a golfer, but it did not come easily. Extremely private, he did not socialize well, which kept him from the networking that helps start careers and move them forward.

And, being small of stature, Hogan developed an extended golf swing in order to create power. He achieved the power but at the expense of accuracy. Hogan's driving, in particular, featured a wild hook that for the first eight years of his professional career (he turned pro at age 18) kept him on the periphery of the tournament circuit. Hogan concluded in subsequent years that the most important shot on any golf hole is the first one, the drive, and he eventually became exceptionally accurate off the tee while retaining sufficient power. What's more, he added to that a stunningly precise approach-shot game that made up for a lifetime of relatively ordinary putting skills.

"The answer to Hogan is, I fancy, that if Hogan means to win, you lose."
—HENRY LONGHURST, ON BEN HOGAN

Hogan often said he figured the golf swing by himself—"dug it out of the dirt," as he liked to put it. He took the idea of practice to an extraordinary level for golfers of his era, and while this surely was an important element in his success, he was also an inquisitive student of the golf swing who picked up ideas on technique from many sources. One of his sources was Henry Picard, a Masters and PGA champion in the 1930s who would become one of golf's best teachers. Picard convinced Hogan that to beat his hook, he had to "weaken" his left-hand grip by turning the hand more to the left. Seemingly overnight, Hogan's basic shot became a left-to-right power fade, a trajectory that came to be known as the "Hogan Fade." The flight pattern would influence how the game would be played from then on.

In early 1940, Picard's lesson hit home. Hogan won his first professional tournament individually, the much-prized North and South Open. (In 1938, he had shared victory with partner Vic Ghezzi in the Hershey Four-Ball.) The next week, Hogan won the Greater Greensboro Open, and later in this "coming out" season he won twice more. After nine years of struggle, during which he more than once had to leave the tournament circuit for lack of funds, Hogan was at last fulfilling his promise. From 1940 to '42, he won 15 tournaments, and in each year he was the Tour's leading money winner. All that was missing on his increasingly impressive résumé was a major title.

Hogan was primed for this breakthrough, but it was put on hold with the advent of World War II. The Tour was discontinued in 1943, and that year Hogan was inducted into the U.S. Army and then assigned to the Air Corps. Like most celebrated athletes serving military duty, Hogan did not see combat. He trained pilots for a time but, for most of his hitch, played exhibitions to raise money for the war effort, played casual golf with high-ranking officers, practiced on his own, and entered the occasional Tour event when the circuit began again in 1944. Still, he was away from steady, high-level competitive golf for 3½ years.

When Hogan returned full-time to the tournament circuit, he made up for lost time with characteristic tenacity. In his first outing after his discharge, in the fall of 1945, Hogan won the Portland Invitational with a record-setting 72-hole score of 261—27 under par. From 1946 through the early part of 1949, playing what he would later describe as the best golf of his life, he won 32 tournaments, including his first and second majors—the 1946 PGA Championship and 1948 U.S. Open.

Then, after playing four events on the 1949 winter circuit and winning twice, Hogan and his wife, Valerie, nearly lost their lives. On a foggy two-lane highway outside Van Horn, Texas, a Greyhound bus traveling in the opposite direction moved out to pass a slow-moving truck and collided head-on with Hogan's car. When Hogan saw the accident coming, he instinctively stretched across the front seat to protect his wife. He saved her from serious injury, and saved his life as well, for at impact the steering column of his car was rammed into the driver's seat. Nevertheless, Hogan's left collarbone was fractured, his left ankle was snapped, and many of his internal organs were severely damaged. His face was smashed into the dashboard, which led to a gradual diminishment of the vision in his left eye. He would intimate, after he retired, that he had essentially played the last three or four years of his competitive golf career with sight in only one eye.

Furthermore, during his recuperation time, Hogan's life was again seriously threatened by a blood clot. A quick operation saved him, but his legs were left in a permanent state of weakness and disrepair. That he survived at all was a wonder. That he would, within a year, return to competitive golf was beyond anyone's farthest consideration. But it soon happened, and in a most dramatic fashion.

In January 1950, Hogan entered his first competition following the accident, the Los Angeles Open, and nearly won it; he lost to Sam Snead in a playoff. But the most astounding moment came in June 1950. In the U.S. Open, which at the time concluded with a 36-hole final day, Hogan barely held on to tie George Fazio and Lloyd Mangrum with a par on the last hole. In the 18-hole playoff the next day, Hogan won the title.

Had he never played competitive golf again, Hogan's extraordinary comeback in 1950 would have been enough to secure his place forever in golf annals. But he would expand on it, and mightily. Cutting back his playing schedule to preserve his strength, Hogan entered an average of only six tournaments a year from 1951 to '53, most of them the majors except for the PGA, which was then a physically grueling match-play event requiring as much as two full rounds a day. Nonetheless, during that period Hogan won eight times, five of them majors—two more U.S. Opens, two Masters, and one British Open in his only attempt for that crown. In 1953 alone, he won what might be called golf's Triple Crown—the U.S. and British Opens and the Masters. He would also play on the U.S. Ryder Cup team, captain the team for a third time, produce an especially influential instructional book—*The Modern Fundamentals of Golf*—and found a golf equipment manufacturing company in his own name.

Hogan won his last tournament—the Colonial Invitational—in 1959. In 1960, at age 48 and essentially retired from competitive golf, he had enough left to be in a position through 71 holes to win his fifth U.S. Open. That he lost did nothing to tarnish a reputation for golf skill and a will to excel that will live through the ages.

CAREER HIGHLIGHTS

Earnings: $207,779
PGA Tour Victories: 63
Achievements: Won 1948, 1950, 1951, and 1953 U.S. Opens; 1951 and 1953 Masters; 1946 and 1948 PGA Championships; 1953 British Open. Led Tour in earnings in 1940, 1941, 1942, 1946, and 1948. Vardon Trophy winner in 1940, 1941, and 1948. PGA Player of the Year in 1948, 1950, 1951, and 1953. Won 13 Tour events in 1946. Member of PGA/World Golf Hall of Fame. Captained the United States Ryder Cup team three times.

HALE IRWIN

○ ○ ○

ONLY FOUR PLAYERS—Willie Anderson, Bobby Jones, Ben Hogan, and Jack Nicklaus—have won more U.S. Opens than the three claimed by Hale Irwin. In fact, along with those four (who won four Open titles apiece), Irwin is the only other player with more than two. He took the national championship in 1974, '79, and '90, in the latter year becoming the oldest player, 45, to take the title.

It is fitting that the U.S. Open, where conditions are most difficult, should represent Irwin's crowning achievement; he has always been at his best on tough courses. Among his 20 PGA Tour victories, he has won on such renowned courses as Harbour Town, Butler National, Riviera, Pinehurst No. 2, Muirfield Village, and Pebble Beach. He is a relatively short hitter, a fine long-iron player, and a tough competitor; he is at his best when par is a good score.

Irwin, a native of Missouri, fueled his competitive drive as a football player at the University of Colorado, where he was an all-conference defensive back. He also won the 1967 NCAA golf championship. Irwin joined the Tour in 1968 and had two career wins before the 1974 U.S. Open. Irwin emerged there, surviving the "Massacre at

Winged Foot," to win with a 7-over-par total. He won his second Open, at Inverness, at even par.

Irwin's third Open win came in very different fashion. He was tied for 20th place, four strokes behind, entering the final round, but closed with a 67 that included a sizzling 31 on the back nine at Medinah. A 45-foot birdie putt on the 18th hole ultimately put him in a playoff with Mike Donald, which Irwin won with a sudden-death birdie on the 19th hole.

Though he didn't win any other majors, Irwin was one of the top players in the game for a long period. He won at least once in all but two years from 1973 to 1985 and finished among the top 10 money winners eight times in his career. He made 86 consecutive cuts from 1975 through '78, the third-best streak in history. A five-time U.S. Ryder Cup player, Irwin is now a dominant force on the Senior Tour and was named 1997 Senior Tour Player of the Year.

CAREER HIGHLIGHTS
Earnings: $5,876,574 (PGA); $4,758,308 (SR)
Tour Victories: 20 (PGA); 13 (SR)
Achievements: Won 1974, 1979, and 1990 U.S. Opens; 1996 PGA Seniors Championship; 1967 NCAA championship. Finished among top seven in PGA Tour earnings each year from 1973 to 1978. Five-time U.S Ryder Cup team member. All-Big Eight defensive back in football while at the University of Colorado.

TONY JACKLIN

AT TWO DIFFERENT TIMES in his life, Tony Jacklin emerged as the man who restored pride to golfers on the eastern side of the Atlantic. In 1969, he became the first British golfer in 18 years to win the British Open (and, the next year, the first in 50 years to take the U.S. Open). Then, at The Belfrey in 1985, he captained the European Ryder Cup team to its first victory over the U.S. in 28 years (and, two years later, its first win ever on U.S. soil).

Born in Scunthorpe, England, Jacklin turned professional in 1961 at the age of 17. He became a strong force in 1967, winning two events in Britain and finishing fifth in the British Open. The next year, he journeyed to the United States to play the PGA Tour and won the Greater Jacksonville Open, in what was the first U.S. Tour victory by a British-based player since Ted Ray won the 1920 U.S. Open.

In 1969, Jacklin became a British hero by winning the British Open at Royal Lytham and St. Annes, beating Bob Charles by two strokes. Jacklin's performance in the 1970 U.S. Open was even more impressive; his seven-stroke victory margin at Hazeltine National was the largest at the Open since 1921.

Jacklin finished fifth, third, and third in the next three British Opens, but, thereafter, ceased to be a factor in the major championships. Some think the 1972 British Open was a fatal blow. He seemed primed to win there until the 71st hole. Tied for the lead with Lee Trevino, Jacklin watched Trevino chip in for a par and then three-putted from 15 feet for a bogey. Jacklin won once more in the U.S., in 1974, and became less of a factor on the European Tour as the decade wore on.

Jacklin, an outspoken and confident sort, found a new role in the 1980s as captain of the European Ryder Cup team. Working with a strong nucleus of players, he instilled a belief that the Europeans could beat the mighty U.S., and, after coming close in 1983, they accomplished the trick in 1985 and 1987.

Jacklin joined the Senior PGA Tour in 1994 and won the First of America Classic that year. He added the Franklin Quest Championship in 1995.

CAREER HIGHLIGHTS
Earnings: $352,179 (PGA); $1,074,694 (SR)
Tour Victories: 3 (PGA); 2 (SR)
Achievements: Won 1970 U.S. Open; 1969 British Open. Captained 1985 European squad to its first Ryder Cup victory in 28 years and the 1987 team to another Cup win. Also captained the 1983 and 1989 squads and played on seven other Ryder Cup teams.

BOBBY JONES

○ ○ ○

THE SUM TOTAL of Bobby Jones's contributions to golf is virtually all-encompassing. As a championship golfer, he set standards that still hold, even if the scores he shot have become irrelevant. He was an excellent and prolific writer on golf—particularly his golf instruction, which has a clarity, intelligence, and warmth of insights that to this day makes good reading. He was the quintessential amateur during his competitive career—an impeccable gentleman (once he "grew up") and true to the code of amateurism. Finally, he gave his game a golf course and a tournament that have become institutions reflecting what has come to be considered the ultimate expression of golf aesthetics and competitive rigor and drama.

Robert Tyre Jones Jr. was born in Atlanta in 1902, the only child of a lawyer who was an inveterate golf buff. Bobby began playing golf at age five, and he was soon deemed a prodigy. For good reason. At nine, Jones won the junior championship of the Atlanta Athletic Club, soundly defeating a lad seven years older than himself in the final match. At 12, Jones won three different club championships, in one shooting a final-round 73. He won the Georgia State Amateur the next year, then played in his first U.S. Amateur, where he took the defending champion, Bob Gardner, on the 31st hole before losing.

With his Amateur showing, Jones impressed one and all with his golf, but not with his temper. He was a club and tantrum thrower, the misbehavior accompanied often by highly "colorful" language. He would ever pleasure in such language when in private and among men friends, but he did lose the tantrum part, which got in the way of his progress as a golfer. In the third round of his first British Open, in 1921, Jones was playing poorly and picked up at the 11th hole without finishing it. It was a breach of good conduct he never forgot, and it had much to do with the princely deportment for which he became renowned.

In view of the tournament schedule of many amateur golfers today, which includes heavy summer schedules and extensive and highly competitive collegiate play, one of the most remarkable aspects of Jones's career was that he played so little competitive golf. He studied mechanical engineering at Georgia Tech, earned a degree in English literature at Harvard, and—after 18 months at the Emory University Law School—took the Georgia state bar examination. He passed it and left school to practice law. He never did play college golf.

Preferring to play himself into condition for each golf season, Jones did not practice much on the range. He only rarely entered amateur events, other than the nationals. He won the Southern

Amateur three times, but he has no record in such long-time prestigious amateur tournaments as the North and South or Western. He did play in two pro Tour events in preparing for his monumental 1930 season: the Savannah Open, which he lost by a shot to Horton Smith, and the Southeastern Open, which he won by 13 strokes after finishing double bogey, par, double bogey. Other than those few instances, the national championships were his only interest, and his metier.

"There are two kinds of golf—golf and tournament golf. The latter is an aging game."
—BOBBY JONES, 1930

During what has been described as his eight "fat years," 1923–30, Jones won the U.S. Amateur five times (and lost once in the final), the U.S. Open four times (lost twice in a playoff), the British Open three times (in four tries), and the British Amateur once (in three tries). He became known as Emperor Jones, and even hard-nosed professionals who managed to beat him in an Open counted it a high achievement, if not an honor.

Jones had a great sense for historic accomplishment, for prior to the 1930 season he resolved to win all four of the then-major golf titles in that one year—the U.S. and British Open and Amateur championships. It had never been done before, and this would be his last chance, for he had also decided that 1930 would be his last year of competitive golf. He had a family to raise, and he never did get over the edgy nervousness that his youthful temper displayed. The physical and emotional stress of his great play over the previous 15 years was taking its toll. Furthermore, the Walker Cup was being played in Great Britain in 1930, which allowed him the opportunity for his goal. Except in one instance, he had only played in Great Britain when representing the U.S. as a Walker Cup player, and the bulk of his travel expenses were covered by the USGA.

And so it came to pass that one of the finest feats of sustained golfing excellence in the history of the game took place: the Grand Slam. Or as one wordsmith of the day phrased it: the "Impregnable Quadrilateral."

It is certain Jones was after the British Amateur crown, for it was the only one of the four majors he had never won. Jones's most anxious moment in the British Amateur, at St. Andrews, was in the fourth round, when Cyril Tolley had a 12-foot birdie putt on the last hole to win 1 up. He missed, and Jones won on the first extra hole after laying a stymie on his foe. Jones breezed in the final, however, clubbing Britain's Roger Wethered, 7 & 6. At Hoylake two weeks later, all ears were tuned to Jones as the British Open was broadcast over American radio for the first time. Jones led the Open through the first three rounds and broke the 72-hole course record by 10 strokes. When he arrived back in the States, New Yorkers honored him with a ticker-tape parade.

On to Minnesota and the U.S. Open, the third leg. At the Interlachen Country Club, Jones took a five-shot lead with a third-round 68—the lowest he had ever shot in the U.S. Open. Nevertheless, he had to birdie three of the last six holes in the final round to win by two over Macdonald Smith. A 40-foot birdie putt on the last green was the clincher.

Given his own momentum, and the undoubted awe everyone had for Jones by the time the U.S. Amateur came around, his victory in that championship was practically assured. Jones won the 36-hole qualifying medal with 69–73. In the matches, he was never down to any opponent, and he clinched the title with an 8 & 7 romp in the finals. Jones then retired from championship golf. He was 28 years old.

Jones, though, would long remain associated with the game. He made a series of instructional films called *How I Play Golf*, wrote several books, and helped design a set of clubs. Working with course designer Alister Mackenzie, Jones also created what would become one of the most famous layouts in the world—the course at Augusta National Golf Club, future home of the Masters.

Jones clearly articulated his criteria for the new course. It would give the average golfer a fair chance, while requiring the utmost from top players. There would be over 300 yards difference between the championship and members tees. But most significantly, the fairways would be wide, there would be no rough, and the course would include only 29 bunkers. The correct placement of shots would be paramount to negotiating the undulating ground. For Jones, golf was mainly a game of control.

Construction began in early 1932, with Jones hitting many shots from the projected tees and fairways to ascertain the proper angles, sight lines, distances, and playability of each hole. Many features of the Old Course at St. Andrews, Jones's favorite, were incorporated into the design. The grand opening was on January 13, 1933. People came from around the world for the unveiling. The weather didn't cooperate but golf was played, and Jones, on January 14, shot a round of 69. Augusta National had been properly christened.

CAREER HIGHLIGHTS

Achievements: As an amateur, won 1923, 1926, 1929, and 1930 U.S. Opens; 1926, 1927, and 1930 British Opens; 1924, 1925, 1927, 1928, and 1930 U.S. Amateurs; 1930 British Amateur. Member of PGA/World Golf Hall of Fame. Winner of all but one 36-hole match from 1923 to 1930. Won his era's Grand Slam in 1930—the U.S. Open, U.S. Amateur, British Open, and British Amateur. Designer of Augusta National Golf Club. Founder of the U.S. Masters, later known as the Masters.

Robert Trent Jones

○ ○ ○

THE MOST PROLIFIC AND INFLUENTIAL golf course architect of the second half of the 20th century, Robert Trent Jones is credited with designing more than 450 courses in 42 states and 23 countries in a career that has stretched over 60 years.

Jones was born in England in 1906 and moved to the U.S. with his parents in 1911. Jones knew early in life what he wanted to do. As a student at Cornell University, he designed his own curriculum of courses that would prepare him for a career in golf architecture. Jones then became a partner of the Canadian architect Stanley Thompson.

Jones's career took off after World War II, when golf began to boom in America. He became known for his redesigns of U.S. Open courses, which he modernized to keep up with advances in golf equipment. The first and most famous of these redesigns came at Oakland Hills in preparation for the 1951 U.S. Open. The course was dubbed "The Monster," and Jones's reputation was established. He remodeled several other Open sites in the 1950s and '60s, and he eventually had three Opens played on courses of his own design: Bellerive, Hazeltine National, and Atlanta Athletic Club.

Jones advocated the philosophy of strategic design, blending the heroic and penal principles of golf architecture. He became known for designing courses with long teeing grounds and large, undulating greens, and he brought water into play more than the architects of past eras. His more famous courses include Spyglass Hill in California, Firestone in Ohio, the Dunes in South Carolina, Peachtree in Georgia, and Mauna Kea in Hawaii. He worked extensively in Europe, where his most acclaimed course is Valderrama in Spain.

Jones, working with chief assistant Roger Rulewich, continued turning out courses as he approached his 90th birthday. The Robert Trent Jones Golf Trail in Alabama, opened in the early '90s, is one of the most ambitious and successful public-course projects in the country. Jones's sons, Robert Jr. and Rees, are respected architects in their own right.

CAREER HIGHLIGHTS

Achievements: Designed more than 450 golf courses in a career of 60-plus years. Redesigned several U.S. Open courses, including Oakland Hills in preparation for the 1951 Open, to help them keep up with advances in equipment. Designed three Open courses himself—Bellerive, Hazeltine National, and Atlanta Athletic Club. His famed Valderrama course in Spain, one of several of his European courses, played host to the 1997 Ryder Cup Matches.

BETSY KING

○   ○   ○

IT TOOK BETSY KING A WHILE to hit her stride on the LPGA Tour, going her first seven years without a victory. Once she came into her own, however, King needed only 12 productive years to put together Hall of Fame numbers.

King's lack of early success on Tour was a bit surprising in light of her amateur record. She finished eighth in the 1976 U.S. Women's Open as an amateur and led her Furman team to the national collegiate championship that year. King ranked among the top 30 money winners five times in her first seven years on Tour, yet she couldn't find the winner's circle.

Finally, three years of work with instructor Ed Oldfield began to pay off. King not only scored her first victory in 1984, but she added two more that year and won the money title and Player of the Year honors. King would again sweep those honors in 1989 and '93, also claiming the Vare Trophy for low scoring average in 1987 and '93. King won at least two tournaments every year from 1984 to '92, and she ranked among the top 10 money winners each year from 1984 through '95.

King won her first major title in the 1987 Nabisco Dinah Shore. She had her best year in 1989, winning six tournaments. The biggest was the U.S. Women's Open at Indianwood in Michigan, where King held or shared the lead after every round. King won the Nabisco Dinah Shore and U.S. Women's Open a second time each in 1990. King's best performance came in the 1992 LPGA Championship, where she came in with rounds of 68–66–67–66 for an LPGA Tour-record 267 total and an 11-stroke victory. It marked the first time in LPGA history a player shot four consecutive rounds in the 60s in a major championship.

As King approached the 30-victory mark required for induction into the LPGA Hall of Fame, the wins became harder to achieve. She finished second five times in 1993 before scoring her only victory, the 29th of her career, in the season's final event. After a winless 1994, King finally scored her 30th win in June 1995 at the ShopRite Classic. That year, she became the first LPGA player to pass the $5 million mark in career earnings.

CAREER HIGHLIGHTS

Earnings: $5,374,022
LPGA Tour Victories: 31
Achievements: Won 1987 and 1990 Nabisco Dinah Shores; 1989 and 1990 U.S. Women's Opens; 1992 LPGA Championship. Tour Player of the Year and top money earner in 1984, 1989, and 1993. Vare Trophy winner in 1987 and 1993. Member of LPGA Hall of Fame.

TOM KITE

○ ○ ○

CONSISTENCY HAS ALWAYS BEEN the hallmark of Tom Kite's game. From week to week and year to year, his performance has seldom wavered. His reward is more than $9 million in PGA Tour earnings, second to Greg Norman on the career list.

Kite came out of Austin, Texas, a year ahead of Ben Crenshaw (they shared the same teacher, Harvey Penick, and also shared the 1972 NCAA Championship). Kite joined the PGA Tour in 1973 and established a pattern by making 31 of 34 cuts. While he was a steady money earner, it took Kite a while to become a winner, with just two victories through 1980.

Kite's breakthrough year came in 1981, even though he won only one tournament. He had a phenomenal 21 top-10 finishes in 26 starts, led the money list, and won the first of two consecutive Vardon Trophies. With the exception of 1988, Kite would win at least one tournament in every year from 1981 through '93, including three in 1989 (when he won his second money title) and two each in 1984, '92, and '93, running his career total to 19 victories. He slipped out of the top 10 money winners only three times in that 14-year stretch.

For much of his career, Kite's only shortcoming was his inability to win a major championship. He finally earned his first in the 1992 U.S. Open, where he shot an even-par 72 on Sunday at Pebble Beach when most contenders were being blown away by severe winds. His best chance before that came in the 1989 U.S. Open at Oak Hill, where he led through three rounds before finishing with a 78. He was a perennial contender at the Masters for a long stretch, with 10 top-10 finishes from 1975 to '86, finishing second in 1983 and '86.

At a slender 5'8", Kite isn't able to overpower courses, though he gets more distance off the tee than his frame might suggest. He has an excellent short game and for much of his career was one of the top putters, but he has struggled on the greens in recent years.

Kite played well for much of 1997, and some felt he merited consideration for the U.S. Ryder Cup team. However, the team captain—Kite himself—decided Kite would only play if he earned one of the 10 automatic spots. He did not.

CAREER HIGHLIGHTS

Earnings: $9,657,325
PGA Tour Victories: 19
Achievements: Won 1992 U.S. Open; 1989 Players Championship; 1989 Tour Championship; 1972 NCAA title. Veteran of seven U.S. Ryder Cup squads before captaining the 1997 team. Tour Player of the Year in 1989. Led Tour in earnings in 1981 and 1989. Vardon Trophy winner in 1981 and 1982.

BERNHARD LANGER

○ ○ ○

BEFORE BERNHARD LANGER, Germany had never produced even a middling professional golfer on the European scene. But Langer, the son of a Bavarian bricklayer, became a world-class golfer, not only becoming the first German to win on the European Tour, but also leading the European Order of Merit twice and winning two Masters titles.

There are few public courses in Germany, but Langer got involved in the game as a caddie at age nine, and by the time he was 15 he went to work as an assistant professional. He hit the European Tour at age 18 in 1976, only to run into a battle with the yips on short putts. They finally abated in 1980, when he claimed his first regular European Tour victory at the Dunlop Masters. Thus began a string of 16 straight years in which Langer recorded at least one win in Europe.

Though his short game is one of his strong suits, Langer has been plagued by periodic putting problems throughout his career. In 1988, he went to a unique putting grip, where he grabbed his left forearm with his right hand. That worked well for a few years, but in 1996, struggling again, he went to a long putter. Nothing has seemed to help him regain his winning touch.

Langer led the Order of Merit in 1981 and '84. In the former year, he won twice, finished second six times, including the British Open, and had 14 top-10 finishes in 17 starts. In 1984, he won the Irish, Dutch, French, and Spanish Opens. He has won the German Open five times.

Langer's first venture into America was the 1981 World Series of Golf, where he led with nine holes remaining before fading. Four years later, he was ready to win a big one. Shooting consecutive rounds of 68 on the weekend, Langer stormed past a field of contenders that included Curtis Strange, Ray Floyd, and Seve Ballesteros to win the Masters. He followed with his second U.S. win the next week at the Sea Pines Heritage Classic. Langer won another Masters in 1993, taking a three-stroke lead with a third-round 69 and winning by that margin over Chip Beck.

CAREER HIGHLIGHTS
Earnings: $2,759,486
PGA Tour Victories: 3
Achievements: Won 1985 and 1993 Masters; 1981, 1982, 1985, 1986, and 1993 German Opens; 1989 and 1991 German Masters. Once went 70 straight tournaments on PGA European Tour without missing a cut. Member of eight European Ryder Cup teams between 1981 and 1993.

TONY LEMA

○ ○ ○

ONE CAN ONLY GUESS what Tony Lema would have accomplished in golf if he hadn't died in a plane crash in 1966 at age 32. It can be said for certain that he was one of the top five players in the world at the time of his tragic death—and one of the game's best personalities.

Lema came from a humble background in Oakland, California. He didn't make much of a mark in his first few years after joining the Tour in 1957, winning three small-purse events that didn't have official status. But things turned around in the fall of 1962, when Lema won three tournaments and earned a nickname. His second win came at the Orange County Open, where Lema led after three rounds and promised the press champagne if he won. When he delivered, he became "Champagne Tony."

In the next three years, Lema finished fourth, fourth, and second on the money list. Though he scored only one victory in 1963, he made a strong run at the Masters, finishing second, one stroke behind Jack Nicklaus. The next summer belonged to Lema. He won three tour events in June, giving him four wins for the year. In July, he headed for the British Open at St. Andrews. It was his first tournament ever in Britain, and he allowed himself time for only one full day of practice. The skeptics scoffed that it wasn't enough time to get to know the idiosyncracies of the Old Course, but Lema simply hit the ball where his caddie told him to, handled the tricky shots around the greens deftly, and cruised to a five-stroke victory over Nicklaus.

Lema nearly defended his British title in 1965, holding the lead after two rounds before falling to fifth place. He won two PGA Tour events that year and finished with $101,000 in earnings, becoming the first player other than Nicklaus or Arnold Palmer to crack six figures in a season. But Lema's life came to a tragic end the next July on the way from the PGA Championship to a pro-am in Illinois.

Lema is also remembered for his brief but successful Ryder Cup career. Playing in the 1963 and 1965 Matches, he registered seven wins and two halves against just one defeat.

CAREER HIGHLIGHTS
PGA Tour Victories: 13
Achievements: Won 1964 British Open. Finished second in Tour earnings in 1965, joining Arnold Palmer and Jack Nicklaus as the only men to win $100,000 in a single season. Won British Open in his first attempt. Posted seven wins, two halves, and one loss in 1963 and 1965 Ryder Cup Matches.

LAWSON LITTLE

○ ○ ○

ALTHOUGH HIS PROFESSIONAL CAREER was considered a disappointment, Lawson Little dominated amateur golf for a two-year stretch more than any player in history except for Bobby Jones. In fact, in winning both the U.S. and British Amateurs in 1934 and '35, Little accomplished a feat unmatched by even Jones.

Little, born in 1910 in Newport, Rhode Island, first attracted attention in the 1929 U.S. Amateur. After Johnny Goodman scored a shocking upset of Jones in the first round, Little beat Goodman in the next round. Little reached the semifinals of the 1933 U.S. Amateur, earning a spot on the U.S. team for the 1934 Walker Cup at St. Andrews. He won both of his matches there, then stayed in Scotland for the British Amateur at Prestwick.

Little's performance in the 1934 British Amateur final was one of the finest days of golf ever played. He won the scheduled 36-hole match by a record margin of 14 & 13 over Jack Wallace, playing 23 holes in 10-under 4s. Returning to America, Little rolled to the U.S. Amateur title in another lopsided final, beating David Goldman, 8 & 7. The margins were closer in the following year's final matches—1 up over William Tweddell in the British Amateur, and 4 & 2 over Walter Emery in the U.S. Amateur. But when the championships were done, Little had won 31 consecutive matches to sweep the world's major amateur titles two years running.

Little turned pro in 1936 instead of trying for what would today be called a "three-peat." He won the Canadian Open that year, but his shining moment as a professional came when he defeated Gene Sarazen in a playoff to win the 1940 U.S. Open at Canterbury Golf Club in Cleveland, Ohio. However, that was the only major he won as a professional, and he collected only eight pro victories in all.

The stocky Little was one of the longer hitters of his day. He was also known for a fine short game, which was helped for a time by carrying as many as 26 clubs before the USGA imposed a 14-club limit.

CAREER HIGHLIGHTS
PGA Tour Victories: 8
Achievements: Won 1934 and 1935 U.S. Amateurs; 1934 and 1935 British Amateurs; 1940 U.S. Open; 1936 Canadian Open. Remains only player in history to sweep both U.S. and British Amateurs in consecutive years. Finished third in 1939 Masters. Member of PGA/World Golf Hall of Fame.

GENE LITTLER

○ ○ ○

HIS RHYTHMIC SWING and unerring accuracy earned Gene Littler the nickname "Gene the Machine." Hailed as one of the game's coming superstars in the mid-1950s, Littler went on to a long and successful career that included 29 PGA Tour victories over a span of 23 years. His only disappointment was that he won only one major championship, the 1961 U.S. Open.

Littler was born in San Diego in 1930 and first made an impact in the game when he won the 1953 U.S. Amateur. Still an amateur in 1954, he won his hometown event on the PGA Tour, the San Diego Open. Shortly thereafter, he turned pro. Littler's "golden boy" reputation was furthered when he finished second in the 1954 U.S. Open, missing an eight-foot putt on the 72nd green that would have gotten him into a playoff, and won four times in 1955. Littler slumped for a couple years, but he had his best year in 1959 with five victories.

The biggest win of his career came two years later, when he took the U.S. Open at Oakland Hills. He came from three strokes behind by shooting a final-round 68. Littler came close in two other majors, losing in playoffs at the 1970 Masters to boyhood friend Billy Casper and the 1977 PGA

Championship to Lanny Wadkins. At the latter event, the 47-year-old Littler was trying to become the second-oldest major-championship winner ever (Julius Boros won the PGA Championship at age 48), but he lost a five-stroke lead on the back nine.

Littler finished among the top 32 money winners every year but one from 1954 through 1975 (ranking second in 1959 and '62). The lone exception was in 1972, when he underwent surgery in the spring for cancer of the lymph glands. He was back in action six months later and won a tournament the next year. In 1975, at age 45, he won three times and finished fifth on the money list. His final PGA Tour victory came at age 47. He has gone on to add eight official and eight unofficial Senior PGA Tour wins.

Littler's international experience is also extensive. He played on the U.S. Ryder Cup team seven times between 1961 and 1975.

CAREER HIGHLIGHTS

Earnings: $1,578,626 (PGA); $2,148,066 (SR)
Tour Victories: 29 (PGA); 8 (SR)
Achievements: Won 1961 U.S. Open; 1955, 1956, and 1957 Tournament of Champions. Lost playoff to Billy Casper in 1970 Masters. Lost playoff to Lanny Wadkins in 1977 PGA Championship. Member of seven U.S. Ryder Cup teams from 1961 to 1975. Member of PGA/World Golf Hall of Fame.

BOBBY LOCKE

◦ ◦ ◦

FEW FOREIGN GOLFERS have had as much impact on American golf as South Africa's Arthur D'Arcy "Bobby" Locke. In fact, no other international player has had such immediate success in the U.S. as Locke enjoyed after arriving in 1947.

Two developments in 1946 encouraged Locke, then age 29, to give the American Tour a try. He finished second to Sam Snead in the British Open, then beat Snead in 12 of 16 matches when the American star went to South Africa for an exhibition tour. Locke racked up six victories in 13 U.S. events in 1947, finishing second on the money list despite not playing the whole season. In 1948, he won twice, one of them by a Tour-record 16 strokes at the Chicago Victory Championship.

The run of victories was startling considering Locke's unorthodox methods. Early in his career, Locke had been a very short hitter; his solution for gaining distance was to hit a pronounced hook off every tee. He practiced very little and believed that American pros were too mechanical with their swings; Locke played by feel. Locke was a brilliant putter, but even on the greens he incorporated a sort of hook stroke.

The American pros resented both his success and the appearance fee he commanded to skip the British Open to play in George S. May's All-American Open in 1947, which he won. Locke also alienated the press by asking for $100 if they asked questions of an instructional nature. Ultimately, the PGA banned him in 1949, saying he had failed to honor commitments. Gene Sarazen called the dismissal "the most disgraceful action by any golf organization in the past 30 years." The PGA reinstated him in 1951, when Locke scored the last of his 10 American victories, but he played very little in the United States after that except for the U.S. Open.

Locke spent the latter part of his career playing mostly in Great Britain, and he won the British Open in 1949, '50, '52, and '57. Though he never won the U.S. Open, Locke finished third there in 1947 and '51, fourth in '48 and '49, and fifth in '54. He won the South African Open nine times and notched 38 total wins in his homeland, including both amateur and professional victories.

CAREER HIGHLIGHTS
PGA Tour Victories: 10
Achievements: Won 1949, 1950, 1952, and 1957 British Opens. Captured six U.S. Tour events in 1947 and finished second in earnings. Won 1948 Chicago Victory Championship by Tour-record 16 strokes. Posted five top-five U.S. Open finishes. Banned by PGA from 1949 to 1951. Member of PGA/World Golf Hall of Fame.

NANCY LOPEZ

○ ○ ○

GOLF IS NOT A GAME CONDUCIVE TO STREAKS. Just making two or three consecutive birdies is something special, and it is rare for a golfer to win just two tournaments in a row. So when someone does streak, it gets a lot of attention. That's what happened to Nancy Lopez in 1978, when she won five events in succession on the LPGA Tour—and nine tournaments in all that year.

The streak hoisted Lopez immediately into the spotlight of big-time golf, and it also was a much needed fillip for the women's tournament circuit, which was having trouble at the time getting attention in an increasingly diverse sports world. Nancy's streak put her, and her organization, indelibly on the sports map. It didn't hurt that she also had one of the most beautiful smiles seen in a public figure, a smile that reflected the natural warmth of her character.

Nancy Lopez was born in 1957 in Torrance, California, but was raised in Roswell, New Mexico. Her father, Domingo, was the driving force behind Nancy's career. He was himself a golfer, and when he recognized Nancy was also interested and had talent, he did all he could to help her go forward in the game. Mr. Lopez made a modest living running an auto repair shop, but he always found the money it took to get his only child the golf equipment she needed—as well as to pay the greens fees at the local municipal course and military base course on which she learned to play.

There wasn't any money for lessons, so Nancy was largely self-taught. The result of this was an unusual, idiosyncratic swing in which she arched her wrists to an almost vertical position to begin her backswing, which was very upright. From there on, however, she had a fine tempo and—with superb control of the club—had a "traditional" downswing and follow-through. Her distance was never outstanding, but she knew how to handle problem shots. Her father didn't give her much swing instruction, but when Nancy was eight he gave her a 4-wood as her first club and encouraged her to not tee the ball up but rather to play the ball as it lay, as she found it. Lopez's soft putting touch, one of the best the game has ever seen, was probably innate.

It came together quickly. When Nancy was 12, she won the New Mexico Women's Amateur championship. That she defeated much older and more experienced golfers goes without saying. She was quickly deemed a golfing prodigy and was invited to play and practice as often as she liked at country clubs in Roswell. She took up the offers graciously, with that marvelous smile. Lopez won the U.S. Girls' Junior championship in 1972 and '74 and the Mexican Women's Amateur in '75.

That same year, she entered her first U.S. Women's Open and tied for second. Within the above time frame, she also fit in three victories in the prestigious Western Girls' Junior championship. In 1976, she played for the U.S. Curtis Cup team and was also on the U.S. World Amateur team. Lopez received a golf scholarship to Tulsa University, but after her sophomore year she turned pro, in 1977.

> *"The pressure makes me more intent about each shot. Pressure on the last few holes makes me play better."*
> —NANCY LOPEZ, GOLF'S MENTAL MAGIC

All the more remarkable for an athlete of her accomplishments, Lopez—the wife of baseball star Ray Knight—found the time and energy to become a mother of three children, and to raise them conscientiously. Her first daughter was born in 1983, her second daughter in 1986. Within those years and up to 1991, when she gave birth to her third daughter (and won a tournament while carrying her), Lopez won 19 tournaments, earned over $2 million in prize money, and had a stroke average of just over 71.

Lopez continued to play a full schedule of tournaments from 1992 to '95, teeing it up in 77 LPGA events, winning three of them, and collecting over $1 million in prize money. In the 1992 Rail Charity Classic, she tied her career-low score, a 64, in the final round to take the title. Through 1996,

Lopez had won 47 official LPGA tournaments (plus three unofficial ones), which ranked her sixth all-time. The only LPGA players to win more often played in the formative years of the Tour, when there were fewer competitors.

In 1987, Lopez was inducted as the 11th member of the LPGA Hall of Fame. But in a curious parallel with Sam Snead, an unquestionably great player who never won the U.S. Open, Lopez has never been able to capture the women's national championship, although she has been runner-up on three occasions. She can't explain that one smudge on her otherwise splendid record, just as Snead couldn't. Nor has Lopez tried very hard to fathom the reason. "Maybe some day," she has said with that incandescent smile, which has defused all further questions on the matter. Some day she may win the Open, but if not she will not be any less a champion.

CAREER HIGHLIGHTS
Earnings: $4,275,685
LPGA Tour Victories: 48
Achievements: Won 1978, 1985, and 1989 LPGA Championships. Captured a record-setting five tournaments in a row among nine overall wins in 1978. Vare Trophy winner in 1978, 1979, and 1985. Rolex LPGA Player of the Year in 1978, 1979, 1985, and 1988. Set all-time record in 1985 Henredon Classic with 20-under-par 268. Member of LPGA Hall of Fame and PGA/World Golf Hall of Fame.

Lloyd Mangrum

○ ○ ○

With his riverboat-gambler looks and stylish game, Lloyd Mangrum was a popular and successful player in the decade after World War II, although he was overshadowed by contemporaries Ben Hogan and Sam Snead. Mangrum ranks 10th all time in PGA Tour victories with 36, collecting 30 of those from 1946 through '54.

Mangrum grew up in Texas and turned pro at age 15 in 1929, but he didn't hit the Tour until the late 1930s. He first made news in 1940 when he scored his first victory at the Thomasville Open and shot a first-round 64 in the Masters (an 18-hole record that wasn't matched for 25 years or broken for 46) before finishing second, behind Jimmy Demaret.

Mangrum joined the Army in World War II and earned two Purple Hearts when he was wounded during the Battle of the Bulge. In 1946, he won the first postwar U.S. Open in a tense play-off over Byron Nelson and Vic Ghezzi. All three players shot 72s in the 18-hole playoff at Cleveland's Canterbury Club, necessitating another 18 holes. Mangrum shot another 72, while the other two had 73s.

In 1948, Mangrum began winning in bunches. He had seven wins that year, then added four in 1949, five in '50, four in '51, two in '52, and four in '53. He led the money list in 1951 and won the Vardon Trophy in 1951 and '53. In 1949, he was part of the longest playoff in PGA Tour history, going 11 holes with Cary Middlecoff at the Motor City Open before darkness arrived and the two were declared co-winners.

The 1946 U.S. Open remained Mangrum's only major victory. His next best chance came in the 1950 U.S. Open, where he and George Fazio lost a playoff to Ben Hogan. Mangrum trailed by one stroke on the 16th green when he lifted his ball to blow a bug off of it. Cleaning your ball on the green was not allowed then, so he drew a two-stroke penalty and ended up losing by four. Mangrum was a perennial contender in the Masters, finishing in the top eight every year from 1947 through '56, including a second-place finish in 1949.

CAREER HIGHLIGHTS

PGA Tour Victories: 36
Achievements: Won 1946 U.S. Open. Led Tour in earnings in 1951. Vardon Trophy winner in 1951 and 1953. Ranks 10th all time in Tour victories. Won seven events in 1948. Finished among top eight in Masters each year from 1947 to 1956. Part of Tour-record 11-hole sudden death playoff in 1949 Motor City Open.

CAROL MANN

○ ○ ○

ONLY FOUR PLAYERS HAVE EVER won 10 or more LPGA Tour events in one year—Betsy Rawls, Mickey Wright, Kathy Whitworth, and Carol Mann. In fact, Mann and Whitworth won 10 apiece in the same year, 1968, leaving only a dozen events for the rest of the players.

That came during a two-year run when Mann made a run at Whitworth for No. 1 status in the women's game. While they were dominating the victory column in 1968, Mann won the Vare Trophy with a record 72.04 scoring average (not broken until Nancy Lopez came along 10 years later) and Whitworth claimed the money title. In 1969, Mann won the most tournaments (eight) and led the money list, while Whitworth claimed the Vare Trophy.

Mann, a native of Buffalo, New York, joined the Tour in 1961 at age 20. Her first win came in what was then considered a major championship, the Western Open. So did her third win, the 1965 U.S. Women's Open. She never won another major event, but for most of her career the LPGA had only two majors, the Women's Open and the LPGA Championship. She was second in the Women's Open in 1966 and '74 and second in the LPGA Championship in 1969. Mann also was runner-up in the inaugural Colgate Dinah Shore in 1972.

Mann was hard to miss on the golf course. She was the tallest woman golfer ever at 6'3" (or, as she liked to joke, 5'15") and had an effervescent personality. She was capable of feats of low scoring. Mann had 23 rounds in the 60s in 1968, a record that stood for 12 years; she made seven straight birdies at the 1975 Borden Classic, a record that stood for nine years; and she had a 54-hole total of 200 at the 1968 Carling Open, a record that stood for 13 years.

Mann finished in the top four on the money list in every year from 1965 to '69, won at least one tournament in every year but one from 1964 to '75, and finished her career with 38 victories and more than $500,000.

A former president of the LPGA, Mann was a key figure in the formation of the modern women's Tour. She is a member of the International Women's Sports Hall of Fame.

CAREER HIGHLIGHTS

Earnings: $506,666
LPGA Tour Victories: 38
Achievements: Won 1965 U.S. Women's Open. Vare Trophy winner in 1968. Led Tour in earnings in 1969. Made seven consecutive birdies in 1975 Borden Classic. President of Women's Sports Foundation from 1985 to 1990. Member of LPGA Hall of Fame and the International Women's Sports Hall of Fame.

JOHN McDERMOTT

○ ○ ○

He would end up spending most of his life in mental institutions, but as a young man John McDermott became the first player born in America to win the U.S. Open and, at age 19, the youngest ever to win the event. From its inception in 1895, the U.S. Open had been dominated by Scottish-born pros before McDermott broke the ice in 1911. McDermott repeated as Open winner in 1912, but three years later, at age 23, he had a nervous breakdown and never competed on the golf course again.

McDermott, who grew up in Philadelphia, entered his first U.S. Open at age 17 and finished 48th. The next year, when the U.S. Open was held at the Philadelphia Cricket Club, he reached a three-way playoff with brothers Alex and Macdonald Smith, losing to Alex. The cocky McDermott predicted a victory in 1911 and he delivered, prevailing in a three-way playoff over Mike Brady and George Simpson.

Desperate to prove his win wasn't a fluke, McDermott traveled to the 1912 British Open but shot a horrible 96 in qualifying and didn't make the field. When he came home, he won his second

U.S. Open with a final-round 71, an excellent score for that era.

In 1913, McDermott finished fifth in the British Open, but when he returned home things began to go wrong. First, he discovered that he had lost heavily in investments. Then he was involved in a controversy when, after beating Englishmen Harry Vardon and Ted Ray in a tournament during their American tour, he said, "We are sure they won't win the National Open." McDermott ended up finishing eighth in the Open—behind Vardon, Ray, and the winner, Francis Ouimet. McDermott's best golf was behind him.

In 1914, McDermott tried the British Open again but had a disastrous trip. He missed a ferry and was late for the qualifying round, declining an official's offer to let him play anyway. Then, on the way back, his ship was involved in a crash, though he was unhurt. McDermott finished ninth in that year's U.S. Open. The next year, he suffered a breakdown, and his career was over.

CAREER HIGHLIGHTS
Achievements: Won 1911 and 1912 U.S. Opens; 1913 Western Open. Became first native-born American to win U.S. Open title at the age of 19 in 1911. Lost in a playoff to Alex Smith in 1910 U.S. Open. Tied for fifth in 1913 British Open. Defeated touring Harry Vardon by 13 strokes to win 1913 Shawnee Open.

Bill Mehlhorn

○ ○ ○

His contemporaries in the 1920s rated Bill Mehlhorn as one of the best strikers of the ball ever, but also one of the shakiest putters. Still, he managed to win 20 tournaments, all of them between 1923 and 1930, and run up a string of high finishes in the U.S. Open. He was given the nickname "Wild Bill," probably because he worked for a time in Oklahoma and liked to wear cowboy hats when he played.

Mehlhorn, born in 1898 of a German immigrant father, actually grew up in the Chicago suburbs, not the Wild West. He quit high school when he was offered a job as an assistant pro. Mehlhorn got his first break as a pro when he was picked for an American team to compete in Scotland against a team from Great Britain; on the same trip, he finished seventh in the British Open. He later played on the first Ryder Cup team in 1927.

Mehlhorn's first two victories came in 1923. The next year, Mehlhorn claimed the Western Open, a tournament that then had major status. He never won the U.S. Open or PGA Championship, though he was a perennial contender in the Open. Mehlhorn finished fourth in 1922 (when he had a share of the third-round lead), eighth in 1923, third in 1924, third in 1926 (falling back after an opening-round 68), fifth in 1927, ninth in 1930, and fourth in 1931. He reached the final of the PGA Championship in 1925, losing 6 & 5 to excellent golf by Walter Hagen.

Mehlhorn's best years were 1926, when he won five times; 1928, with six wins; and 1929, with four. When his putting was on, he was capable of phenomenally low scoring for the day; his 271 total for 72 holes at the 1929 El Paso Open was a record. However, stories of his putting problems were legion. Once, it was said, he had a three-foot birdie putt and yipped it clear off the green. Another legend has "Wild Bill" turning a short putt into a bunker shot. Mehlhorn's winning days ended after 1930, though he made it to the semifinals of the PGA Championship as late as 1936.

It was said Mehlhorn's putting stroke improved later in life, too late for it to help earn him more pro victories. The rest of his game was always solid.

CAREER HIGHLIGHTS
Achievements: Won 1924 Western Open. Posted U.S. Open finishes of third in 1924 and 1926; fourth in 1922 and 1931; and fifth in 1927. Lost to Walter Hagen in final match of 1925 PGA Championship. Represented United States against Great Britain during matches in 1921, 1926, and 1927.

Cary Middlecoff

○ ○ ○

Walter Hagen once called Cary Middlecoff one of the best ball-strikers ever to come out of American golf. Middlecoff won two U.S. Opens (1949 and 1956) and lost another (1957) in a playoff against Dick Mayer. He won one Masters title (1955) and had two seconds at Augusta National. He reached the finals of the 1955 PGA Championship and in all had 40 wins from 1945 through '61, which puts him in a seventh-place tie for all-time Tour wins with none other than Hagen. Middlecoff also had 30 second-place finishes, 23 thirds, and 181 top-10s. His first important victory came in the 1945 North and South Open, an auspicious accomplishment in that he was an amateur at the time and still a lieutenant in the U.S. Army.

Emmett Cary Middlecoff was born in 1921 in Halls, Tennessee, the son of a dentist. He attended the University of Mississippi and played on the school's golf team, then went into the military during World War II, serving as a dentist. Middlecoff would share his father's practice on and off for a time after his discharge from the Army, but he was encouraged by his father to give professional tournament golf a try. "Doc" Middlecoff joined the pro Tour full-time in 1947, but he would occasionally work at dentistry to keep up his skill should the golf not work out. As it happened, after 1948, he never filled another cavity other than those on golf courses.

A tall, slender man, Middlecoff had an intense, nervous manner that seemed unsuited for a game that prizes calm and patience. But he found a way to counter his nature, purposely developing a swing technique that distinguished him from the great majority of golfers—a distinct pause at the top of his backswing. Middlecoff was also one of the more deliberate players in the game, fidgeting over the ball at address for some time before beginning his swing. Joked writer Dan Jenkins: "A joke on the Tour used to be that Cary gave up dentistry because no patient could keep his mouth open that long." Actually, Middlecoff's slow play was mainly because of physical problems that plagued him for most of his career.

Middlecoff gave up his dental practice and, a year and a half later, won the U.S. Open. "I was enough of a neophyte not to know what I was doing," he said. "I found out it was harder after that."

Middlecoff was born with an extra lumbar vertebrae. And while in dental school, standing for long periods in a dentist's position, he developed back problems. Golf exacerbated the condition. He also had trouble with his left eye, the result of a piece of Carborundum coming off a disc while treating a patient in the Army. It hit him in his left eye, which became ulcerated and was never the same again. He always wore a green visor on the golf course to kill the glare of the sun. On top of the physical problems, Middlecoff suffered from hay fever, beginning in 1955. "One of the main reasons I took a lot of time over the ball was that I couldn't see very well," Middlecoff recalled. "The hay fever was part of it, and the problem with the left eye was also a factor." Finally, he had to give up the game in the 1960s when he couldn't control the yips.

Middlecoff was always described as a "streaky" player, punctuating stretches of relatively ordinary golf with rounds—if not weeks and years—when he was at the pinnacle of his profession. For example, in winning his one Masters title, he outdistanced the second-place finisher, Ben Hogan, by seven shots. In winning his first U.S. Open, he bunched his best play—a second-round 67, a third-round 69—to take a three-shot lead into the last 18 holes. In defending his U.S. Open crown in 1957, Middlecoff got hot with two 68s in the last two rounds to force a playoff with Mayer. The 136 total tied a record for the final 36 holes of the championship.

On a bigger scale, Middlecoff in 1951 became a member of an elite group of golfers—including Hogan, Byron Nelson, Sam Snead, and Arnold Palmer—when he won three consecutive events. He also had a knack for sustaining excellent, winning golf over a full year. In 1949, he won seven times, including a dramatic U.S. Open in which he fended off Snead and Clayton Heafner by one stroke. He won six times in 1951 and matched that record again in 1955. Middlecoff played on three U.S. Ryder Cup teams (1953, '55, and '59) and in 1956 won the Vardon Trophy for low scoring average with a stroke average of 70.35. Middlecoff's last victory, at the Memphis Open, came in 1961 in his hometown. As an author, he wrote the insightful books *Advanced Golf* and *The Golf Swing*.

For all his obvious high achievements, Middlecoff was not sufficiently recognized as the golfer he was. This may be due in part to the fact that he was in his prime when Hogan and Snead were dominating American golf. Be that as it may, Middlecoff's outstanding record speaks for itself. He was listed as the ninth-best American golfer of all time, according to the 1989 PGA Tour rankings.

CAREER HIGHLIGHTS

Earnings: $295,168
PGA Tour Victories: 40
Achievements: Won 1949 and 1956 U.S. Opens; 1955 Masters. Vardon Trophy winner in 1956. Member of PGA/World Golf Hall of Fame. Holed an 86-foot eagle putt during his 1955 Masters win. Finished second in Tour earnings four times. Won seven Tour events in 1949 and six in 1951 and 1955. Posted 181 top-10 tournament finishes.

JOHNNY MILLER

○ ○ ○

JOHNNY MILLER FIRST CAME to national attention as a golfer in the 1966 U.S. Open, at the Olympic Club in San Francisco. A tall, slender, blond 19-year-old with an exciting style, he put on a fine show of golf on national television as he finished as low amateur and in a four-way tie for eighth place. That he had the advantage of being a member of the Olympic Club was only coincidental. Miller looked the part of a "comer" on golf's biggest stage, and indeed he would become one of the game's lead players.

Born in 1947 in San Francisco, John Laurence Miller was directed into golf by his father at an early age. Under the tutelage of teaching professional John Geertsen, Miller developed a swing technique that would be adopted by a number of star players who came after him—an "early set," in which he cocked his wrists very early in the takeaway and then completed his backswing. It made him one of the most accurate iron players the game has ever had. In 1964, Miller won the U.S. Junior Amateur championship, then went on to play college golf at Brigham Young University. In 1968, he won the highly competitive California Amateur title, then the following year turned professional and joined the PGA Tour.

Miller's third victory as a pro was the 1973 U.S. Open. It was an outstanding accomplishment in itself, especially at so early a stage in his career, and Miller did it in stunning fashion, shooting a phenomenal and historic final round of 8-under-par 63 on the very difficult Oakmont C.C. course. Rains had softened the layout, making the greens more receptive than usual, but a 63 in a U.S. Open had never before been achieved. It brought Miller from six shots off the 54-hole pace to win by a single shot, and it made him an instant star.

> **"Serenity is knowing that your worst shot is still going to be pretty good."**
> —JOHNNY MILLER

The following year, Miller solidified his status by winning eight events on the PGA Tour. Of his total 24 career PGA Tour victories, eight would be in Arizona and Palm Springs, California (Phoenix Open twice, Tucson Open four times, Bob Hope Classic twice), in some cases with exceptionally low scores. Two of his Tucson victories came with 72-hole totals of 263 and 265. As a result, he was categorized as someone who played his best only in the "desert." In fact, the so-called "Desert Fox" won nationwide and worldwide and on a geographically wide spectrum—Florida, the Carolinas, northern California, New York, Pennsylvania, and Europe.

Miller's second major title was the 1976 British Open, at Royal Birkdale in England. His best showings in other majors were two near-misses in the Masters. In 1971 at Augusta, Miller had a two-stroke lead after 68 holes but went 4-over the rest of the way to finish in a tie for second with Jack Nicklaus. Charles Coody won. Then, in 1975, Miller fired a brilliant final-round 66 and needed a birdie on the last hole to tie Nicklaus. It was one of the more thrilling of Masters, but it was not to be for Miller. He tied for second with Tom Weiskopf.

There was a notable gap in Miller's victory production from 1977 to '79, when he won nothing on the PGA Tour and only once abroad. Many felt his attention had been distracted by the many endorsement and exhibition opportunities that came his way after making his mark. Indeed, he was one of the first modern-day professional golfers to become an agent-directed off-course commodity. But Miller also involved himself deeply in raising a large family (six children, all two years apart), and he was beginning to suffer from a neurological problem with his knees that would gradually deteriorate to where he could play only occasionally, and then with great discomfort. So bad had Miller's physical problem become that in 1988 he was unable to defend his AT&T Pebble Beach National Pro-Am title.

Miller would make up for that in a most fascinating and sentimental way. From 1990 to 1993,

Miller entered only six tournaments, and in 1994 he signed up for the AT&T if only for old times' sake; he loved playing on the Monterey Peninsula, had won the event twice, and wanted to give his older sons, who had high golfing aspirations, a chance to compete on this level. But it was Dad who took the limelight. He shot a third-round 67 to move one stroke out of the lead with a round to play. And although he struggled in the final round under difficult weather conditions, his 74 was good enough to win by a stroke. If it is the last of Miller's wins, it was a beautiful way to go out.

Miller began doing color commentary for NBC in the late 1980s, and almost immediately he became a highly popular, albeit sometimes controversial, figure. With his articulate, insightful analyses of golf technique, he surprised many with how much he understood about the mechanics of the swing.

CAREER HIGHLIGHTS

Earnings: $2,746,424
PGA Tour Victories: 24
Achievements: Won 1973 U.S. Open; 1987 and 1994 AT&T Pebble Beach National Pro-Ams; 1974, 1975, 1976, and 1981 Tucson Opens. Led Tour in earnings in 1974, joining Jack Nicklaus and Tom Watson as the only money title winners between 1971 and 1980. Eight-time winner and Tour Player of the Year in 1974. Member of PGA/World Golf Hall of Fame. Two-time U.S. Ryder Cup team member.

Old Tom and Young Tom Morris

○ ○ ○

No father–son tandem has ever matched Tom Morris Sr. and Jr., who each won four British Opens in the early days of competitive golf. Old Tom is still the oldest ever British Open winner, at 46 in 1867, and Young Tom is the youngest, at 17 in 1868. The two finished 1–2 in the 1869 British Open, with Morris Jr. prevailing over his mentor.

When Old Tom was young, he served as an apprentice clubmaker and ballmaker under Allan Robertson of St. Andrews, who was considered the best player of the day. The two formed a nearly unbeatable team in challenge matches against other Scottish duos. Morris, however, split with Robertson in business when Morris was quicker to accept the replacement of the old featherie golf ball with the gutta percha. In 1851, Morris Sr. left St. Andrews to become the custodian of the new links at Prestwick (Young Tom was born that same year).

In 1860, the Open Championship was begun to determine Scotland's best golfer. Old Tom was runner-up to Willie Park in the first Open, then won in 1861, '62, '64, and '67. Morris Sr. returned to St. Andrews as pro and greenkeeper in 1865 and remained there until his death in 1908.

Young Tom, considered the most powerful player of the time, took the mantle from his father, winning the Open in 1868, '69, and '70, shooting a then-phenomenal 149 for 36 holes at Prestwick to win by 12 strokes the latter year. Young Tom's third straight victory gave him permanent possession of the champion's belt, and there was no competition in 1871. The next year, when the tournament resumed with a trophy as the prize (the same one awarded today), Young Tom won for the fourth straight time.

Morris Jr. finished third and second in the Open in the next two years. In 1875, his wife died during childbirth and the baby also did not survive. Young Tom never recovered from the shock, and he died three months later at age 24.

CAREER HIGHLIGHTS
Achievements: Tom Sr. won 1861, 1862, 1864, and 1867 British Opens. Tom Jr. won 1868, 1869, 1870, and 1872 British Opens. The duo finished 1–2 in 1869 British Open. Tom Sr. remains the oldest Open champ at 46; Tom Jr. is still the youngest at 17. Old Tom served as pro and greenkeeper at St. Andrews. Young Tom died at age 24. Both are members of PGA/World Golf Hall of Fame.

BYRON NELSON

○ ○ ○

MANY PERFORMANCE RECORDS are set in sports, and most are invariably broken. One, however, may well stand the test of time. That is Byron Nelson's streak of 11 straight victories on the PGA Tour, in 1945. The skein may never be topped not only because of its immensity, but because it would take a golfer who could play better than Nelson. There have been a few as good—Jones, Hogan, Snead, Nicklaus—but none better. The streak was the work of an all-time master golfer.

John Byron Nelson Jr. was born in Fort Worth, Texas, in 1912. He was one of three children of a grain and feed merchant, and he grew up in a house beside the Glen Garden Country Club, where Byron began caddying at age 10. A fellow caddie, born the same year, was Ben Hogan.

In his first caddie tournament, Nelson shot 118 "not counting the whiffs," as Byron recalled. The next year, he shot 79. "I just fell into it," said Byron, when asked how he got so good so fast. He was also the recipient of sound instruction early on from the club pro, Ted Longworth, and his assistants, Dick and Jack Grout. The latter would be Jack Nicklaus's lifelong golf mentor.

In 1930, Nelson won his first important tournament, the Southwest Amateur. But he "came up" in the heart of the Depression, and he couldn't afford to play amateur golf. In the casual manner of the day, he turned pro in 1932. "Ted Longworth started a tournament in Texarkana, where he was now the pro," Nelson recalled. "The total prize money was $500, and there are people playing in it like Dick Metz and Ky Laffoon—established players—but I rode a bus over there carrying my little Sunday bag and suitcase, paid my $5 entry fee, and played in my first tournament as a pro. All you had to do then was say you were playing pro, and that was it."

Nelson finished third, won $75, and was encouraged. But he soon found himself struggling to make a living and took a job as professional at a golf club in Texarkana. He lived in a boarding house, saved his money, and practiced. "Very seldom did anybody come to the club before noon on any day," he said. "There was an excellent practice field, so I hit balls. I hit 'em down, then hit 'em back. So I got better and better."

He made a couple of forays on the pro Tour in 1933 and 1934, driving a Model-A Ford roadster. The first time out, he came back nearly broke. In '34, he did a bit better, but when offered a job as assistant pro at a fine club in New Jersey, he decided to take it. At about that time, steel shafts had taken over from hickory, and Nelson found he had to make major changes in his technique to adapt to them. He is credited as being the first important golfer to design a golf swing specifically for steel shafts: a more vertical action that, with irons especially, produced crisper, more accurate shots.

In 1936, Nelson won the Metropolitan Open, a PGA sectional (New York–New Jersey) event but one in which such golfing luminaries as Craig Wood, Paul Runyan, and Tommy Armour—also club pros in the area—competed. It was the equivalent of a full-fledged PGA Tour event. Nelson was on his way.

"At my best, I never came close to the golf Byron Nelson shoots."
—BOBBY JONES

In 1937, Nelson won the Masters, and in doing so gave first evidence of his proclivity for streaks of hot golf. With seven holes to play and four shots behind the leader, Nelson birdied the par-3 12th, eagled the par-5 13th, and parred in to pass Ralph Guldahl. (When he won the 1945 PGA Championship, during his fabled "streak," Nelson was two down with four holes to play in his second-round match against Mike Turnesa. He birdied the 33rd and 34th holes, eagled the 35th, and won, 1-up.)

After his '37 Masters victory, Nelson was chosen to play on that year's U.S. Ryder Cup team, indicating he was now one of the game's "establishment" players. He secured that place all the more in 1939 when he won the prestigious North and South Open, the Western Open, and the U.S. Open. In the latter, he hit one of the most memorable shots in golf history. In the final playoff round, on the long par-4 4th, Nelson drilled a 1-iron second shot into the hole for an eagle-2. A stunning shot, it reflected one of Nelson's greatest attributes as a golfer—phenomenal accuracy.

In 1940, Nelson won three tournaments. One was his third major, the PGA Championship, in which he was one down to Sam Snead with three holes to play in the final and birdied two of the last three to win, 1-up. From 1941 through '44, Nelson won 14 tournaments (eight of them in '44), including another Masters. Then came The Streak.

Nelson was rejected from military service during World War II owing to a blood deficiency, and it has been said that his run of victories in 1945 was not against the toughest possible fields. Hogan and Jimmy Demaret, in the Navy at the time, played in only two of the "streak" events. However, Snead had been discharged from the Navy with a back problem, and he played in all but three of them.

In any case, stroke-play golf is essentially played against the course, and Nelson played them awfully well. During The Streak, he played 38 rounds of stroke play (we omit the first victory, a four-ball in which he had a partner, as well as the match-play formatted PGA Championship), which included two 18-hole playoff rounds against Snead to decide the Charlotte Open. Throughout The Streak, Nelson went round in 2,581 strokes for an average of 67.92 per round. In those 38 rounds, he was 113-under-par. Highlights? Nelson won the Iron Lung Open with a score of 263, a Tour record for 72 holes. In winning the Philadelphia Inquirer Invitational, he birdied five of the last six holes to win by a stroke.

Another demur regarding The Streak has been that Nelson enjoyed the advantage of preferred lies in the fairways at a few events, because not all the courses were in the best condition owing to shortages of machinery and materials during the lean war years. By contrast, however, Nelson also had to putt on greens that contrasted to those on the modern-day Tour; it's like comparing two-lane country roads to a new interstate highway. What's more, as Nelson once remarked, "back then you couldn't repair pitch marks or clean your ball on the greens."

There is simply no getting around it. Nelson's streak was an unmatchable exhibition of sustained excellence. Ironically, The Streak was ended when an amateur, Freddie Haas Jr., won the Memphis Invitational. But the next week, Nelson won again, then six more times for a total of 18 victories on the year, which itself is a record that still holds today and may well hold equally as long as the 11 in a row.

Exhausted by his efforts, Nelson said after the '45 season that he was retiring from competitive golf. However, before making it final, he won six times in 1946 and won his last tournament in 1951, when he was 39. He then became an important teacher in the careers of Ken Venturi and Tom Watson, to name but two of his students, then a golf television analyst for many years. And beyond that, he was a warm, unpretentious ambassador for the game.

Because he played his best before the PGA Tour had become as popular as it would, and before television began extensive coverage of it, Nelson's talent at golf was not exposed as widely as was that of his contemporaries, Hogan and Snead, who were born in the same year. But those who saw him ply his trade knew what Nelson had. He had everything.

CAREER HIGHLIGHTS

Earnings: $190,256
PGA Tour Victories: 52
Achievements: Won 1937 and 1942 Masters; 1939 U.S. Open; 1940 and 1945 PGA Championships. Vardon Trophy winner in 1939. Associated Press Male Athlete of the Year in 1944 and 1945. Led Tour in earnings in 1944 and 1945. Won a record 11 consecutive tournaments in 1945, when he won 18 overall Tour events. Won inaugural Dallas Open in 1944, later renamed Byron Nelson Classic. Member of PGA/World Golf Hall of Fame.

LARRY NELSON

○ ○ ○

PRACTICALLY ALONE among today's professional golfers, Larry Nelson did not even play the game until he was an adult. His first golf swings came when he made a trip to the driving range at age 21, after serving a stint in Vietnam. Nelson showed a quick aptitude for the game, breaking 100 over the first 18 holes he ever played. He turned pro just two years after taking it up and qualified for the Tour two years after that. He had played only one 72-hole event before making it to the Tour in 1974.

Nelson was a steady money winner in his first five years, then scored his first two victories in 1979 when he finished second in earnings. He never ranked better than 10th after that, but he developed a reputation for playing his best on the big occasions and on difficult courses. His 10 career victories included three majors—the 1981 and '87 PGA Championships and 1983 U.S. Open. A quiet man, Nelson was nonetheless a steely competitor. The strength of his game has always been accuracy, though he was adequately long as well. If anything kept him from winning more tournaments it was his putting—and the fact that from

1983 on he cut down his schedule in order to spend more time with his family.

Nelson won the 1981 PGA in his hometown by a comfortable four strokes at Atlanta Athletic Club (he also won two Atlanta Classics during his career). In the 1983 U.S. Open at Oakmont, he finished with rounds of 65 and 67, setting a tournament record for the lowest final 36 holes. He was tied with Tom Watson when rain suspended the final round. On his first hole Monday morning, the 16th, Nelson drained a 60-foot birdie putt and went on to win by one stroke. Nelson's win at the 1987 PGA Championship came in a sudden-death playoff over Lanny Wadkins in the heat of PGA National near Miami.

Nelson, who joined the Senior PGA Tour in 1997, also had a strong record in Ryder Cup play. He won all nine of his Matches in 1979 and '81, finishing with a 9–3–1 career record after one more appearance in 1987.

CAREER HIGHLIGHTS
Earnings: $3,625,363 (PGA); $503,096 (SR)
PGA Tour Victories: 10 (PGA); 6 (SR)
Achievements: Won 1981 and 1987 PGA Championships; 1983 U.S. Open; 1979 Western Open. Finished second to Tom Watson in 1979 Tour earnings, winning two events while adding two seconds and two thirds. Posted 9–3–1 record for U.S. team in 1979, 1981, and 1987 Ryder Cups.

JACK NICKLAUS

○ ○ ○

JACK NICKLAUS EXPERIENCED a rather cruel and unfair welcome to the major-league golf scene. How he handled it indicated that this was a man of great self-control and confidence, and one that had the instincts of a gentleman. All of these traits would become implicit as time went on, as Nicklaus would become one of the most dominant golfers in the history of the game.

When Jack Nicklaus won the 1962 U.S. Open, at historic Oakmont Country Club near Pittsburgh, it was his first victory as a professional. However, this superb achievement was clouded by the fact that he defeated Arnold Palmer in a playoff for the title. Palmer was at the height of his game and seemingly invincible as a player, and with his common-man, boy-next-door manner, he had reached an incredible popularity among the golfing public. Nicklaus, on the other hand, was rather overweight and had the air of a pampered country club golfer. Indeed, as everyone knew, he did grow up in a private club setting.

Thus, when he defeated Palmer rather handily in the playoff, not only outplaying but outhitting Palmer off the tee, he was treated with disdain.

How dare he do this to "our Arnie?" Nicklaus suffered many sly indignities from galleries as well as some outwardly rude references to his weight. But through it all, Nicklaus never complained about the treatment. He took it in stride. As he did in his golf, he wore everyone down and brought everyone to his side with his consistently outstanding golf and superb sportsmanship. He was a champion in every way.

When Nicklaus romped to victory at the 1965 Masters, Bobby Jones remarked that Nicklaus was playing a game "with which I'm not familiar." Jones was no doubt referring to the height of Nicklaus's shots with the long irons, which in fact enthralled everyone. They had an unusually high trajectory, the balls seeming to hang forever in the air before landing softly. They also carried astonishingly in their distance. But Jones, a most astute as well as articulate observer of a game he himself had mastered like few others, also had in mind Nicklaus's exceptional putting touch on fast greens as well as a level of poise under pressure that was incredible for so young a man. What would make these attributes all the more exceptional was the length of time that they persisted.

Jack William Nicklaus was born in 1940 in Columbus, Ohio, the son of a pharmacist who at one time owned a small chain of local drugstores. Young Jack had good genes for athletics, as his father had been a fine athlete in a number of games. Jack got quality instruction from the very start. His teacher was Jack Grout, who had been a fine player and became an even finer instructor. And he learned to play on one of golf's better championship layouts, the Donald Ross-designed Scioto C.C., where the Nicklauses were members.

Nicklaus showed he had the stuff of great golf almost from the day he took up the game, at age 10. Three years later, he shot a 3-under-par 69 at Scioto. It only got better. Much better. Nicklaus won five consecutive Ohio State Junior championships, beginning at age 12, and when he won the 1959 U.S. Amateur, at 19 years and eight months, he was the youngest winner of the championship in 50 years. The '59 Amateur came down to the last (36th) hole of the final. Nicklaus needed a nine-footer to close out 35-year-old Charlie Coe, who had twice won the title. He drilled it into the center of the cup. For all his prodigious length off the tee, that kind of clutch putting within the 15-foot range (and sometimes much longer) was perhaps the most distinguished characteristic of his game throughout all his competitive years.

While a student at Ohio State University, and No. 1 on the golf team, Nicklaus won another U.S. Amateur, in 1961. That year he also won the NCAA Championship, the Western Amateur, and the Big Ten championships; played Walker Cup golf; and finished fourth in the U.S. Open. Having conquered the amateur golf world, he turned pro.

His first outing as a regular on the PGA Tour, the Los Angeles Open in January 1962, was in retrospect curiously inauspicious. He finished well down the list and won less than $100. He continued to struggle through the winter while getting used to the travel—a new town and bed every week, restaurant food daily—and playing on the heavily trafficked public-fee courses that were not in the kind of condition to which he had become accustomed. On the other hand, he finished in the money in all 26 events entered and eventually won three times, including his historic U.S. Open. From that point on, he would set competitive records that may well never be matched.

"He plays a game with which I'm not familiar."
—BOBBY JONES, ON JACK NICKLAUS

In the next 25 years, Nicklaus won 67 more tournaments on the PGA Tour (including six Masters, four U.S. Opens, and five PGA Championships) and 18 abroad (including three British Opens). His 20 major titles, including the two U.S. Amateur titles, are seven more than anyone else. Even the greatest of athletes do not win every competition they enter, and in golf that is especially the case. The next and perhaps more meaningful measure, then, of a player's talent is how close he has come to winning those times in which he doesn't in fact walk away with the victory. In this, Nicklaus is far and away the champion of champions. From 1962 to '69 on the PGA Tour alone, he finished in the top 10 in 122 out of 186 events entered and was second 24 times. From 1970 to '79, he was in the top 10 in 111 of 171 events and was second 20 times.

To refine this aspect of his record even more, from 1962 through '79—in a total of 335 PGA Tour events—Nicklaus missed the cut a mere nine times. More to the point, in the major championships in which he made the cut from 1962 to '79, Nicklaus's average finishes were sixth in the Masters, 11th in the U.S. Open, fifth in the British Open, and eighth in the PGA.

Nicklaus set many scoring records along the way. His 271 at the 1965 Masters smashed Ben Hogan's tourney record by three shots, and Jack won the tournament by nine. At the 1967 U.S. Open, Nicklaus drained a 22-foot birdie putt on the 72nd hole to break Hogan's Open record. The 275 mark stood until 1980, when Nicklaus, age 40, shot a 272. Jack's greatest year was 1972, when he prevailed in the Masters, U.S. Open, and five other Tour events; he lost the British Open by a stroke.

The years 1962–79 were essentially Nicklaus's prime years, but he would retain his incredible competitiveness beyond the time when most athletes, great or otherwise, are contenders. He had been the youngest to ever win the Masters, and in 1986 he became the oldest winner of that title (at

46). In the final 10 holes, the old man recorded six birdies and an eagle.

Playing a limited number of events on the Senior PGA Tour, Nicklaus won 10 times (out of 32 tries) from 1990 to '95, twice winning the U.S. Senior Open. And in 1996, playing in his 40th consecutive U.S. Open—itself a record—on the monstrous Oakland Hills C.C. course, Nicklaus finished in a tie for 27th with the same score (287) that Hogan made to win the Open on the same layout. When he strode up the 18th fairway to conclude his play, Nicklaus was greeted with a thunderously warm ovation.

Nicklaus has "officially" and unofficially been dubbed the greatest golfer in the history of the game. Based on his record, and with longevity a definite part of the equation, the designation can hardly be denied.

CAREER HIGHLIGHTS

Earnings: $5,500,051 (PGA); $2,446,648 (SR)

Tour Victories: 70 (PGA); 10 (SR)

Achievements: Won two U.S. Amateur titles; 1963, 1965, 1966, 1972, 1975, and 1986 Masters; 1962, 1967, 1972, and 1980 U.S. Opens; 1966, 1970, and 1978 British Opens; 1963, 1971, 1973, 1975, and 1980 PGA Championships. Won at least one Tour event in 17 straight years from 1962 to 1978. Led Tour in earnings and scoring average eight times. PGA Tour Player of the Year seven times. Associated Press Athlete of the Decade for the 1970s. Member of PGA/World Golf Hall of Fame.

GREG NORMAN

○ ○ ○

Throughout his career, Greg Norman has been an enigma. Winner of about 70 tournaments worldwide and over $10 million in prize money on the U.S. PGA Tour alone, Norman still may go down in the game's annals for how many majors he lost and how he lost them.

In 1986 alone, Norman held the lead in all four of the majors going into the final round of play, yet he won only one of them, the British Open. He is also the only golfer in history to have lost a playoff for each of the majors ('84 U.S. Open, '87 Masters, '89 British Open, '93 PGA). In the 1996 Masters, his collapse in the final round was one of the most astonishing of them all. He shot a course–record-tying 63 in the first round, then—with a six-shot lead going into the final round—shot a 78 to finish second, five shots behind Nick Faldo. It was the largest lead ever "blown" in the last round of a major. Yes, it's been a star-crossed career for Norman, full of amazing highs and amazing lows.

Born in the mining town of Mount Isa in Queensland, Australia, in 1955, Gregory John Norman was by his own description a "skinny, scrawny" youth. Self-conscious of his physique and bound to overcome it, his first athletic interests were in the contact games—rugby, Australian rules football, cricket, squash, and particularly swimming and surfing. He also worked diligently at weight lifting to develop his body. He did indeed become an impressive physical specimen—just over six feet tall, weighing 180 pounds, with broad shoulders, a trim waist, and strong legs. He developed an aggressive, power-oriented golf game that would be adored by the golfing public.

> "Greg is one of the classiest ever to play this game. That's why he's so popular with all the other players, even when he beats us."
> —PETER JACOBSEN ON GREG NORMAN, GAME DAY

Norman did not take up golf until he was 16. His father, a mining engineer, did not play much, but Norman's mother was a three-handicap golfer. While caddying for his mother, Norman decided to hit a few to see what it was like. He was a longball hitter from the start, and with that as the carrot he took up the game. Within two years, he went from a 27 handicap to a scratch golfer, and he became a significant factor in Australian amateur golf. He turned pro in 1976 and began competing on the Australian Tour. He then spread his wings to play the international circuits.

From 1977 through '82, "The Shark" won at least one tournament every year, including such prestigious titles as the Australian Open, Australian Masters, French Open, and Dunlop Masters. In his first U.S. Masters, in 1981, he finished a very respectable fourth, only three shots off Tom Watson's winning score and one behind runners-up Jack Nicklaus and Johnny Miller.

In 1984, Norman began spending more time on the U.S. PGA Tour, where that year he won the Kemper and Canadian Opens. He also was in a playoff for the U.S. Open, where he exhibited for the first time a tendency to self-destruct under ultimate pressure. Three shots behind Fuzzy Zoeller with nine holes to play, Norman drew even after 17 holes. He drove well on the 18th, but his 6-iron approach was pushed some 40 yards right of the green into a grandstand. After a free drop, he managed to save his par (4) with an incredible 45-foot putt over severely undulating terrain. In the playoff, though, he was overwhelmed, 67–75.

In the 1986 Masters, Norman's proclivity to fail at the moment of truth reared up again. Needing a par-4 on the last hole to tie Nicklaus, he hit a 4-iron approach far right of the green and bogied the hole to finish tied for second. Three months later, he won his first major, the British Open, by five strokes. But the following month, he let Bob Tway back into the PGA Championship, shooting a final-round 76 to give up a four-shot lead with 18 to play and setting the stage for Tway's smashing finish.

The pattern was settling in. Norman would either win big, dominating the field, or, more often, let others catch him with his mediocre to poor play. He lost the 1987 Masters when Larry Mize holed a 45-yard chip shot in sudden death.

Through all the shocking defeats and collapses, even as he has cut back his overly aggressive game management, Norman has maintained a calm public demeanor. He simply points to his overall record, which is indeed remarkable. Over 14 seasons through 1997 on the U.S. Tour, he posted more than 100 top-10 finishes, including 18 victories, and won the Vardon Trophy three times. Of course the money has followed. In 1995 alone, he set a PGA Tour season record for money won, with $1,654,959. He soared to No. 1 on the career money list despite playing a limited schedule.

And yet, he is found wanting. A golfer of his ability is supposed to win more majors. He shrugs at the notion and says he will just keep trying. Of that, we can be sure.

CAREER HIGHLIGHTS

Earnings: $10,484,065
PGA Tour Victories: 18
Achievements: Won 1986 and 1993 British Opens; 1994 Players Championship; 1984 and 1992 Canadian Opens. First Tour player to reach $10 million in earnings. Vardon Trophy winner in 1988, 1989, and 1994. Led Tour in earnings in 1986, 1990, and 1995. Tour Player of the Year in 1995. Owner of eight runner-up finishes in majors, including a playoff loss in each.

Francis Ouimet

○ ○ ○

Francis Ouimet wasn't a completely untried and unknown golfer when he achieved his monumental U.S. Open victory in 1913. The 20-year-old Boston boy was the current amateur champion in Massachusetts, a state with some of the game's best players at the time, and two weeks earlier he had reached the second round of the U.S. Amateur championship before losing to the eventual winner. Still, for Ouimet it was like coming out of nowhere to win a playoff over Harry Vardon and Ted Ray.

There was enough wonderful coincidence in Ouimet's victory to fill a romantic heart to the fullest. Ouimet grew up a pitch-shot distance from the site of his achievement, The Country Club in Brookline, Massachusetts, where he began his golf career as a caddie. He was a modest, polite, tallish young man with a studious air. And, perhaps most significant of all, he was an amateur who not only beat two of the best players in golf in a head-to-head contest, but they were professionals to boot. In those years, amateurs were far more highly regarded than pros. Pro golfers were considered mere mercenaries and were treated not unlike second-class citizens; for instance, they were not allowed into the clubhouses of private clubs. And, of course, Ouimet was an American defeating the lords of British golf.

Ouimet was the first amateur to win the U.S. Open and only the second native-born American to do so. The positive repercussions of Ouimet's victory could never be measured precisely, but there is little doubt that it led to a far wider interest in golf in the United States.

Ouimet's success was no fluke. In winning the 1913 Open, he staged a rally in the fourth round to force an 18-hole playoff. He dominated in the extra round, posting a 72 to Vardon's 77 and Ray's 78. In 1914, Ouimet opened his defense of the U.S. Open crown with a 69, only one shot back of the leader and eventual winner, Walter Hagen. Ouimet ended up tied for fifth. Two weeks later, Francis won the U.S. Amateur championship, trouncing by a whopping 6 & 5 margin the man who had defeated him the year before in that event, four-time champion Jerry Travers.

A serious student of swing technique, and an early investigator of the mental side of golf, Ouimet continued to play at a high level for some 20 years. In 1920, he won the North and South Amateur, a championship that was a close second to the U.S. Amateur in prestige. That same year, he went to the finals of the U.S. Amateur, defeating Bobby Jones in the semifinals before losing to

Chick Evans. As evidence that he had crafted a masterful long-term golf game, Ouimet made a spirited try for the U.S. Open in 1925, finishing only one stroke off the winning total posted by Jones and Willie Macfarlane. In 1931, 17 years after his U.S. Open triumph, he won his second U.S. Amateur, defeating Jack Westland in the final by 6 & 5.

"Francis, be sure to keep your eye on the ball."
—10-YEAR-OLD CADDIE EDDIE LOWERY'S ADVICE TO FRANCIS OUIMET ON THE FIRST TEE OF AN 18-HOLE PLAY-OFF FOR THE 1913 U.S. OPEN

It was not quite his last hurrah. The next year in the Amateur, Ouimet shot a 30 on the first nine of his first match and went to the semifinals before losing to a future U.S. Open champion, Johnny Goodman. Ouimet played on the first nine U.S. Walker Cup teams (beginning with 1922's unofficial meeting through 1934), was the playing captain on the last two teams, and was nonplaying captain four times afterwards.

Ouimet was also the catalyst for what became a more progressive reading of the Amateur Code. In 1916, Ouimet was banned from amateur competition because of an interest he had in a sporting goods store in Boston. The USGA apparently felt he was cashing in on his celebrity status as a golfer. Nothing could be farther from the truth. Ouimet was a devoted advocate of amateur golf, and he had spurned opportunities to truly cash in by playing exhibitions for money and endorsing products. The ban caused an angry furor for what was deemed a too-narrow amateur status stance, and also because the soft-spoken, affable Ouimet was much loved by the golfing public. The USGA more or less sidestepped the controversy in 1918, after he was inducted into the U.S. Army. The USGA used this event to lift the ban and reinstate Ouimet's amateur status.

Not one to hold a grudge, Ouimet would later serve for many years on the USGA's Executive Committee. In time, the USGA, with some input from Ouimet, would soften its Amateur Code. Such was the esteem in which Ouimet was held in the world of golf that, in 1951, he became the first American to be honored as the captain of the Royal & Ancient Golf Club of St. Andrews, Scotland. He died in 1967.

Career Highlights

Achievements: Won 1913 U.S. Open; 1914 and 1931 U.S. Amateur; six Massachusetts Amateur Championships. Was the first amateur to win the U.S. Open and the second native-born American to do so. In 1951, became first non-Briton elected captain of the Royal & Ancient. Member of PGA/World Golf Hall of Fame. Had a stamp dedicated to him by U.S. Post Office.

ARNOLD PALMER

○ ○ ○

It is the rare athlete who achieves a level of popularity that transcends his sport and becomes a national folk hero. Such was the case with Arnold Palmer. His rise to such heights was the result of a unique combination of elements. When Palmer won the 1960 U.S. Open, with an exhilarating final-round 65, the national network telecasting of golf was just beginning to take hold. The conclusion of his great round was seen by millions, who also saw in the author of that remarkable finish a refreshingly animated athlete responding with an obvious, visor-tossing exhilaration that golf fans had not seen before.

What's more, the way Palmer played the game had an endearing quality with which the mass of average golfers could identify. He swung hard and fast and had a less than classic, gyrating follow-through. He hit the ball with great authority and for great distance, and he did not play with the stolid caution of golfers past. Palmer took chances, "went for broke," and the crowd loved him for it. They created what came to be called "Arnie's Army," loyal followers who chased after and cheered him through his prime and even after he was well past his most effective years as a competitive golfer.

Had Palmer not also been a winner, all his charismatic charm would have been little more than an interesting sidebar to golf. But he was a winner, a big winner. By 1960, Palmer had already won 13 tournaments on the PGA Tour, including the first of the four Masters he would capture. The '60 Open victory at Cherry Hills Country Club in Denver had the stuff of which legends are made.

The final round was played on Saturday afternoon. During lunch, Palmer asked companions, "I may shoot 65. What would that do?" "Nothing," said golf writer Bob Drum. "You're too far back." "The hell I am," Palmer snapped. "A 65 would give me 280, and 280 wins Opens."

Three times Palmer had tried to drive the 1st green, and three times he had failed. That afternoon, Palmer went for it again. He hit a smoking tee shot, his ball bounded through a belt of rough fronting the green, and it rolled onto the putting surface 20 feet from the hole. It was a 346-yard clout. He birdied that hole, and five more on the front side, to turn in 30, and a hero was born for the ages.

Earlier in that same monumental season, Palmer had won his second Masters. When he entered the British Open, the world of golf was excited by the possibility of the first modern-day Grand Slam—victories in the four major championships (the PGA would be the fourth leg). He came up one shot shy of the winner at St. Andrews, Kel Nagle, but in merely going to the British Open he revived interest in the grand, old event, an interest that had flagged in previous years because the dominant American stars regularly bypassed it. With the game's history in mind, Palmer conscientiously sought to bring the British Open back to its rightful place in golf. He did that, by dint of his play and his personal appeal, and the game should be eternally grateful to Palmer for this one of his many contributions to it.

"He is the boldest of all players. The game has never seen one like him. The epitaph on his tombstone ought to read: 'Here lies Arnold Palmer. He went for the green.'"
—MARK MCCORMACK, ARNIE: THE EVOLUTION OF A LEGEND

Arnold Daniel Palmer was born in 1929 in Latrobe, Pennsylvania. His father, known as "Deke," was the greenkeeper at Latrobe Country Club and later became its head professional. A good golfer himself—although lame in one leg from having polio as a youth—the elder Palmer was a hard-driving man who demanded the best from his only son, whom he taught to play when Arnold was three years old. The lesson was simple: Eschew "classic" form if it didn't come naturally. Take the club back slowly and then hit the ball as hard as you can. There were times in his career when Palmer considered altering his swing to make it more fluid and graceful, but he would inevitably go back to his roots and rock and sock it even when it seemed to cost him victories.

For example, Palmer's bold style of play was counted as the reason he lost the 1966 U.S. Open, at the Olympic Club in San Francisco. Palmer had a seven-shot lead over Billy Casper with only nine holes to play. Rather than play carefully and nurse his huge lead, he continued to fire away, because that was his way and also because his mind was on breaking the U.S. Open record score of 276. He needed to par the last six holes to do that, but he instead went 6-over to finish in a tie with Casper. He lost in the playoff, again after building up a substantial lead early but giving it up with his slash-and-burn style of golf. But Palmer's golf swing and how he used it reflected his true daredevil character, which is why he was so admired by golf fans, win or lose.

Palmer played some amateur golf prior to turning pro, and he showed promise. He entered Wake Forest University on a golf scholarship arranged by his best friend, Buddy Worsham, younger brother of the 1947 U.S. Open champion. Arnie won the Southern Intercollegiate title in 1950, twice went to the semifinals of the prestigious North and South Amateur, and won the celebrated All-American Amateur at Chicago's Tam O'Shanter Country Club by nine shots over the formidable Frank Stranahan.

But Palmer's ascent in golf was slowed by the tragic death of his friend Worsham, who was killed in a car accident. Palmer dropped out of school, joined the Coast Guard, and when discharged took a job as a paint salesman. He did keep up his golf, though, and—once past the pain of Worsham's death—got back in gear. In 1954, Palmer won the U.S. Amateur championship at the Country Club of Detroit. He would always say that this was the toughest victory of his career, owing to the match-play format. Later that year, Palmer turned professional with the intention of playing the tournament circuit. He never did hold a club job, but he did come to own the golf club where he grew up as well as the Bay Hill Golf Club in Orlando, where he annually hosts the PGA Tour's Nestlé Invitational.

Through 1996, Palmer ranked fourth in PGA history for total victories, with 60. His four Masters came every other year from 1958 through 1964, and all were won in grand fashion. In 1958, Palmer eagled the 67th hole to give him the edge he needed. In 1960, he birdied the last two holes to edge Ken Venturi by a stroke. In '62, he fired a sizzling 31 on the back nine of a playoff to win by three. And in '64, he romped to a six-shot victory.

Palmer's most productive stretch of golf came from 1960 through '63, when he won 29 tournaments. He also won 19 international events, including two British Opens (1961 and '62), and 10 Senior PGA Tour tournaments, including the

U.S. Senior Open (1981). He is tied with Jack Nicklaus for the most consecutive years winning at least one tournament (17), and he was the first golfer to reach the $1 million mark in career prize money. Palmer also holds the record for most Ryder Cup Match victories, with 22. He played on six U.S. Ryder Cup teams and was twice the captain.

Moreover, with his trim waist, muscular arms and upper body, and power-game style, Palmer changed the perception nongolfers somehow had of the game—that it was not athletic. That, along with his ready smile, an unpretentious manner that projected easy access by the gallery (he became known for never passing up an autograph request), and a readiness to talk openly with the press whenever asked, would make Arnold Palmer a household name—golf households and otherwise.

CAREER HIGHLIGHTS

Earnings: $1,904,673 (PGA); $1,634,966 (SR)
Tour Victories: 60 (PGA); 10 (SR)
Achievements: Won 1954 U.S. Amateur; 1958, 1960, 1962, and 1964 Masters; 1960 U.S. Open; 1961 and 1962 British Opens. Vardon Trophy winner in 1961, 1962, 1964, and 1967. Won at least one PGA Tour title in 15 straight years from 1955 to 1969. First Tour player to earn $1 million. Led PGA Tour in earnings in 1958, 1960, 1962, and 1963. Associated Press Athlete of the Decade for the 1960s. Member of PGA/World Golf Hall of Fame. Owns record 22 Ryder Cup Match victories.

COREY PAVIN

○ ○ ○

THOUGH FAR FROM THE MOST TALENTED player of his generation, Corey Pavin has been one of the game's most tenacious competitors. The California native led the money list in 1991, has ranked among the top eight money winners five times, and counts the 1995 U.S. Open among his 14 career victories.

As an amateur, Pavin was an All-American at UCLA and a Walker Cup player. After failing in his first try for his PGA Tour card, he headed overseas and won two European Tour events and the South Africa PGA Championship in 1983. Pavin qualified for the PGA Tour in 1984 and proceeded to win at least one tournament in each of his first five years. He went into a bit of a slump from 1988 through 1990, but rebounded strongly in 1991 and remained one of the top players in the game through 1997.

Pavin scored a pair of wins in 1991, both in playoffs, plus two seconds and two thirds as he claimed the money title. He also had a multiple-win year in 1995, winning the Nissan Open in Los Angeles for the second straight year and claiming his first major. His victory in the former event made him the second player ever to win back-to-back at Riviera Country Club. Ben Hogan was the other. Pavin emerged from a tightly packed bunch of contenders in the U.S. Open at Shinnecock Hills by shooting a final-round 68, wrapping up the victory with a magnificent 4-wood to five feet on the 18th hole.

That is one of many clutch shots for which Pavin is remembered. He has a knack for holing shots in key situations, including an 8-iron on the 72nd hole of the 1992 Honda Classic to reach a playoff (which he won) and a chip shot on the 18th hole of an important Saturday Match in the 1995 Ryder Cup. In three Ryder Cup Matches (1991, '93, and '95), Pavin has amassed an 8–5 record.

Pavin, the last player to win the money title with less than $1 million, doesn't have a textbook swing and, at 5'9" and 150 pounds, doesn't generate a whole lot of distance. But over the years he has developed a reputation as one of the game's finest shot-makers and one of the best at holing pressure putts.

CAREER HIGHLIGHTS
Earnings: $8,026,843
PGA Tour Victories: 14
Achievements: Won 1995 U.S. Open; 1994 and 1995 Nissan Los Angeles Opens. Became fifth Tour player in history to break 260 with 259 (21-under) in 1988 Texas Open. Led Tour in earnings in 1991. Posted 8–5 record for U.S. team in 1991, 1993, and 1995 Ryder Cups.

HENRY PICARD

○ ○ ○

HE WAS ONE OF THE BEST players in the game during the 1930s, but Henry Picard is also remembered for his generosity. In 1937, Picard gave a driver to a young Sam Snead, telling him the one he was using wasn't suited to his game. Snead credited it with turning his game around and used the club for more than 20 years. Picard also offered financial assistance to Ben Hogan when Hogan was down to nearly his last dollar. Hogan later dedicated a book to Picard.

Picard was born in Massachusetts in 1907 and moved to South Carolina when he was 17. He scored his first Tour victory in 1932 and another two years later. Then his game blossomed. Picard won five tournaments in 1935 and led the Masters by four strokes after two rounds before fading to fourth place.

Three more victories followed in 1936 and four in 1937. His two wins in 1938 included one at the Masters, where Picard beat Harry Cooper and Ralph Guldahl by two strokes. Picard's best year came in 1939, when he recorded victories in eight tournaments and was the Tour's leading money winner.

Picard won the 1939 PGA Championship in dramatic fashion over Byron Nelson. Henry was 1 down going to the 36th hole, where both players nearly drove the green on a short par-4. Nelson chipped to 12 feet and then missed, and Picard made his birdie from four feet to square the match. On the first extra hole, Picard hit his drive under a truck. After getting relief, Picard hit his approach shot to seven feet. He made the birdie putt and won the championship when Nelson missed a birdie try from five feet.

Picard had one of the best swings of his day and was a fine long-iron player. He finished his career with 26 Tour victories, 20 of them coming from 1935 through '39. He tired of competition after those peak years, cutting back his schedule starting in 1940 even though he was still playing well. He settled into the life of a club professional and respected instructor, scoring his last Tour win in 1945.

CAREER HIGHLIGHTS
PGA Tour Victories: 26
Achievements: Won 1938 Masters; 1939 PGA Championship; 1934 North and South. Led Tour in earnings and won eight events in 1939. Member of U.S. Ryder Cup teams in 1935, 1937, and 1939. Ranks 19th all-time in Tour victories. Broke or equaled par in 50 of 54 tournaments during one 1930s stretch.

GARY PLAYER

○ ○ ○

IF NOTHING ELSE, GARY PLAYER could have gone down in golf history as the most widely traveled champion of all time. However, it is generally agreed that even if he didn't have to put a million or so miles on his personal odometer, he would still have had his extraordinary career in major-league competitive golf. All professional golfers, by definition, must play on the road. Player's globetrotting was just more extensive and gave his record a little different twist.

Gary Jim Player was born in 1935 in a suburb of Johannesburg, South Africa, but he was raised in that nation's capital. Despite being small and slight of build, he stood out in numerous "physical" sports—cricket, rugby, soccer, track, swimming, and diving—and even as an adult seemed no bigger than a jockey compared to almost all the golfers he outplayed in winning every major championship in the game at least once. He is one of only four to have done so, which puts him in the company of Ben Hogan, Jack Nicklaus, and Gene Sarazen.

Player took up golf at age 15 at the behest of his father, himself a good player. Gary was hooked on the game from the start, a romance that may also have had to do with his meeting the girl who would become his wife. Her father, Jock Verwey, was a well-known golf professional in Johannesburg. Player would work for him as an assistant pro.

Early on, Player had an unorthodox and rather bizarre golf swing, in large part the result of feeling that he had to hit the ball as hard as possible to make up for his size. Yet, he did well at the highest level, an indication of his innate talent as well as a competitive zeal to sustain that talent. In 1956, Player won his first South African Open (he won 13 in all) as well as a tournament on the British Tour. He also finished fourth in the British Open that year.

Player then went about the process of altering his overly strong grip and long and complicated swing, and almost immediately he began his rise to the top of the heap. Interestingly, he did not lose any power. Pound for pound, he was one of the longest hitters in the game, and he was his own best example of the advice he has always given youngsters starting up in golf: First learn to hit the ball for distance, which will always stay with you, then learn to golf the ball for score.

Recognizing that the U.S. PGA Tour was the ultimate training (and proving) ground for big-time golf, Player in 1957 began traveling regularly to play in the United States. In 1958, he won his first American Tour event, the Kentucky Derby Open, and also turned in a second-place showing in the U.S. Open.

In 1959, Player won the first of the three British Opens he would capture. In 1961, he won three times on the U.S. Tour, including his first Masters to become the first foreign player to win that championship. In that Masters, a main feature of Player's golf would come to the fore. On the last day, playing to a delicate pin position from the greenside bunker on the 18th hole, he got down in two for a 280 total. A few minutes later, Arnold Palmer made a 6 from almost the identical spot in the same bunker to finish in a tie for second. In practicing bunker shots, Player would often stay at it until he had holed at least one, sometimes more.

"If I had to choose between my wife and my putter, well, I'd miss her."
—GARY PLAYER

Player's reputation had now grown to such an extent that he, along with Palmer and Nicklaus, were considered golf's "Big Three." That was in part a bit of promotional wizardry by the agent handling all three players, but it was still pretty close to reality. From 1961 to '74, Player would win 17 times on the U.S. Tour, including one more PGA Championship ('72), two more Masters (1974 and '78), and a U.S. Open ('65). In all, he won 21 times on the U.S. circuit. He also won the Australian Open seven times and the World Match Play championship five times, and he was twice the individual winner of the World Cup. On the Senior PGA Tour, Player won 18 times from 1985 through 1995, a tribute not only to the quality of the game he put together years earlier and which he never stopped adapting, but to the superb physical condition that he always maintained.

Through much of Player's career, he was a red flag for people protesting, often quite vigorously, the infamous policy of apartheid that was long extant in his country. He invariably handled it with admirable diplomacy, and he made a point to invite such black golfers as Lee Elder to play at the South African PGA Championship and other tournaments in Player's homeland before the racial policy there was dissolved. In this, Player has contributed to golf in a way more valuable than his competitive record.

CAREER HIGHLIGHTS

Earnings: $1,822,886 (PGA); $4,478,607 (SR)
Tour Victories: 21 (PGA); 18 (SR)
Achievements: Won 1961, 1974, and 1978 Masters; 1959, 1968, 1974 British Opens; 1962 and 1972 PGA Championships; 1965 U.S. Open; 1986, 1988, and 1990 PGA Seniors Championship; 1987 and 1988 U.S. Senior Opens; 1987 Senior Players Championship. Last player to win three consecutive PGA Tour events (1978). Led Tour in earnings in 1961. Member of PGA/World Golf Hall of Fame.

NICK PRICE

○ ○ ○

It took Nick Price a while to find the winning touch on the PGA Tour, but once he did he dominated like no one had since Tom Watson in his heyday. From 1992 to '94, Price won 11 PGA Tour events and five international titles for a total of 16 victories. Three of the victories came in major championships.

Though Price turned out to be a late bloomer, for a while he looked like an early prodigy. The Zimbabwean won the Junior World in San Diego in 1974, claimed his first South African event at age 22 in 1979, and won in Europe the next year. At the 1982 British Open, he led on the final nine before playing the last six holes in 4-over-par to finish second to Watson at Royal Troon. The next year, his first on the PGA Tour, he won the World Series of Golf.

Then, for the next eight years, Price went winless on the PGA Tour. He had five runner-up finishes and ranked between 22nd and 43rd on the money list every year from 1986 through 1990, but he couldn't quite put everything together in one week. He finished second in the British Open again in 1988, this time falling to Seve Ballesteros's closing round of 65. Things finally changed in 1991, when Price won the GTE Byron Nelson

Classic and Canadian Open. His confidence boosted, and putting better than he ever had before, Price was ready to embark on a sustained roll.

He won twice in the U.S. in 1992, including his first major, the PGA Championship at Bellerive in St. Louis. Price had four PGA Tour wins in 1993—the Players Championship in March and three straight starts in the summer. He was even better in 1994, winning five times in just 19 events on the PGA Tour plus finally capturing the British Open with a one-shot victory at Turnberry. With his six-stroke romp in the PGA Championship at Southern Hills, Price became the first player to win two straight majors since Watson in 1982. He also became the first player to win two majors in one year since Nick Faldo in 1990. Price passed the $1 million mark in earnings in 1992, '93, and '94, leading the money list the latter two years. He won the Vardon Trophy in 1993 and again in 1997.

CAREER HIGHLIGHTS

Earnings: $7,740,586
PGA Tour Victories: 15
Achievements: Won 1992 and 1994 PGA Championships; 1994 British Open; 1993 Players Championship; 1991 and 1994 Canadian Opens. Vardon Trophy winner in 1993 and 1997. Led Tour in earnings and won Tour Player of the Year honors in 1993 and 1994. Won six titles and two majors in 1994.

JUDY RANKIN

◎ ◎ ◎

UNTIL 1976, NO WOMAN HAD WON $100,000 in a season on the LPGA Tour. Judy Rankin smashed the barrier that year by earning $150,734, starting a two-year run in which she was the dominant player in the women's game. Rankin won six tournaments in 1976 and five more in 1977, sweeping Player of the Year, Vare Trophy, and money list honors in each year. Rankin's reign ended suddenly when Nancy Lopez took the Tour by storm in 1978–79, and Rankin's career came to an end only a few years later due to back problems.

Judy Torluemke (her maiden name) was a teenage sensation, winning the Missouri Amateur at age 14 and finishing as the low amateur in the 1960 U.S. Women's Open at age 15. She turned pro in 1962 at the tender age of 17. It took until 1968 for Rankin to break into the winner's circle, though she ranked among the top 10 money winners in 1965 and '66.

From 1970 to '79, Rankin scored 25 of her 26 career victories and finished in the top 10 on the money list in every year but one. She earned her first Vare Trophy in 1973, when she had four victories.

Rankin had finished second in the inaugural Colgate Dinah Shore Winner's Circle in 1972, the first big-money tournament in women's golf. Four years later, she won the Dinah Shore, setting up her successful run at a $100,000 season. Her scoring average actually improved in 1977 (from 72.25 to 72.16), when she set an LPGA record with 25 top-10 finishes, though her earnings dipped to $122,890.

Rankin managed only one win each in 1978 and '79, and those were to be her last victories. Unable to swing without pain, she quit the Tour after the 1983 season. Rankin didn't officially win a major, but she won two tournaments that were later designated majors by the LPGA Tour—the Colgate Dinah Shore in 1976 and the Peter Jackson Classic in 1977. She was second in the 1972 U.S. Women's Open and the 1976 and '77 LPGA Championships.

Rankin served as captain of the victorious 1996 U.S. Solheim Cup team, and she was named captain again for the U.S. squad in 1998.

CAREER HIGHLIGHTS
Earnings: $887,858
LPGA Tour Victories: 26
Achievements: Won 1959 Missouri Amateur at age 14. Won seven events in 1976 and set single-season Tour earnings then-record of $150,734. Vare Trophy winner in 1973, 1976, and 1977. LPGA Player of the Year in 1976 and 1977. Set Tour record in 1977 with 25 top-10 finishes in one season.

BETSY RAWLS

○ ○ ○

UNDOUBTEDLY THE BEST GOLFER in history to graduate from college Phi Beta Kappa with a degree in physics and math, Betsy Rawls won 55 events in her LPGA Tour career. Four of those came in the U.S. Women's Open, a record she shares with Mickey Wright.

Rawls started playing golf when she was 17. Four years later, in 1949, she won the first of two straight Texas Amateur titles. After completing her studies at the University of Texas, Rawls decided her future was in professional golf, even though the LPGA Tour was just getting off the ground and purses were low.

Rawls's first victory came in the 1951 U.S. Women's Open, where she finished five strokes ahead of Louise Suggs. Jackie Pung was the victim in both of Rawls's next two Women's Open victories. In 1953, Rawls won an 18-hole playoff, 71–77. Pung was an apparent winner in 1957, but she was disqualified for signing an incorrect scorecard, handing the victory to Rawls. Rawls won her fourth Open in 1960 thanks largely to a third-round 68, which tied the existing 18-hole record.

Rawls won four other major titles: the Western Open in 1952 and 1959 and the LPGA Championship in 1959 and 1969. She won at least one tournament in every year from 1951 through 1965, and she claimed her last victory in 1972 at the age of 44. She won 10 events in 1959, a single-season total bettered by only Wright, and led the money list in 1952 and '59. She won the Vare Trophy in 1959, the same year she set a single-season earnings record ($26,744) that stood until 1963.

Not an exceptionally long hitter, Rawls's strength was her touch around the greens. Her career victory total ranks fourth on the all-time LPGA list behind Wright, Kathy Whitworth, and Patty Berg. She won multiple events every year from 1951 through 1962

After she retired from competition in 1975, Rawls became active in tournament administration. She was the LPGA's tournament director from 1976 to '81 and then became the executive director of the McDonald's Championship. In 1980, she became the first woman to serve on the rules committee for the men's U.S. Open.

CAREER HIGHLIGHTS

Earnings: $302,664
LPGA Tour Victories: 55
Achievements: Won 1951, 1953, 1957, and 1960 U.S. Women's Opens; 1952 and 1959 Western Opens; 1959 and 1969 LPGA Championships. Vare Trophy winner in 1959, when she took 10 titles. Led Tour in earnings in 1952 and 1959. Member of LPGA Hall of Fame and PGA/World Golf Hall of Fame.

JOHNNY REVOLTA

○ ○ ○

IN A FIVE-YEAR SPAN during the 1930s, Johnny Revolta was one of the game's most consistent competitors. In 1935, he finished in the top 10 in 22 tournaments, winning five and finishing second in seven more. He led the money list with a whopping total of $9,543 in the midst of the Great Depression.

Revolta grew up in Wisconsin and turned pro at the age of 18 in 1929. After such impressive feats in regional events as shooting 270 for 72 holes to win the 1931 Minnesota Open and defeating Gene Sarazen and Tommy Armour when they visited during an exhibition tour, he was urged to take his game to the national circuit in 1933. He scored his first victory that year at the Miami Open.

Revolta had 18 top-10 finishes in 1934, though his only two wins came close to home at the St. Paul Open and Wisconsin Open. The next year, he was the best player in the game. His five victories included the Western Open, then a major title, and the PGA Championship.

At the 1935 PGA in Oklahoma City, the 24-year-old Revolta's most noteworthy matches were against veteran opponents. In the first round, he met 43-year-old Walter Hagen, a five-time PGA champion. Although Hagen's winning days were just about over, he was still a threat, and had won the qualifying medal. Revolta, known for a deadly short game, got up and down from bunkers on two of the last four holes to preserve a 1-up victory. Revolta's opponent in the final was 39-year-old Armour, winner of three major championships. Revolta jumped on top early and held the advantage all the way, winning 5 & 3. In the 31 holes of the final, he had no three-putts and one-putted 13 times.

After a lackluster year in 1936, Revolta again made his mark the next two years with a total of six wins and 31 top-10 finishes in 1937 and 1938. He continued to compete through the mid-1940s but couldn't quite recapture his earlier form, winning his last tournament in 1944 at the Texas Open.

Career Highlights

PGA Tour Victories: 18
Achievements: Won 1935 PGA Championship; 1935 Western Open. Led Tour in earnings in 1935 and finished second in 1938. Won five events in 1935. Won matches against Walter Hagen and Tommy Armour en route to 1935 PGA Championship title. Member of U.S. Ryder Cup team in 1935.

CHI CHI RODRIGUEZ

○ ○ ○

GROWING UP IN A POOR FAMILY in Puerto Rico, Juan "Chi Chi" Rodriguez began his long road to golf fame and fortune at the age of nine by swinging at tin cans with a limb from a guava tree. Ed Dudley, the pro at the local course, gave Rodriguez a job as a shoeshine boy, then as caddie master, and fostered the enthusiastic youngster's development as a player. At 17, Rodriguez, who took his nickname from his favorite baseball player, finished second in the Puerto Rico Open. He then joined the U.S. Army and began saving money for a shot at the PGA Tour.

Rodriguez made it to the Tour in 1960, at age 24, and scored his first victory three years later. Though he stood 5'7" and weighed 130 pounds, Rodriguez took a ferocious swing and hit the ball reasonably far off the tee. He was also one of the game's finest shot-makers, able to work the ball left-to-right or right-to-left at will and to get out of trouble with a variety of imaginative shots.

Chi Chi also became known for entertaining the galleries with his quips and antics, which included putting his hat over the hole after making a putt and wielding his putter like a sword in celebration. He toned down his act slightly after a few leading pros persuaded him that it was sometimes distracting to fellow players, but he remained a fan favorite and continues his popular theatrics on the Senior Tour.

Rodriguez finished his Tour career with eight victories, enjoying his best year in 1964 when he had two wins and was ninth on the money list. He ranked among the top 50 money winners in every year but one from 1963 through '74.

Rodriguez's game blossomed on the Senior Tour, which he became eligible for late in 1985. He led the money list in 1987 when he won seven tournaments, including the PGA Seniors Championship, and finished in the top three 14 times. In his first six senior seasons, he won 20 times. Rodriguez is also known for his work for charitable causes, particularly the Chi Chi Rodriguez Youth Foundation.

CAREER HIGHLIGHTS

Earnings: $1,037,105 (PGA); $6,068,903 (SR)

Tour Victories: 8 (PGA); 22 (SR)

Achievements: Won 1972 Byron Nelson Classic; 1973 Greater Greensboro Open; 1987 PGA Seniors Championship; 1986 Senior Players Championship. Won Digital Seniors Classic three straight times (1986 to 1988). Member of 1973 U.S. Ryder Cup team. Member of PGA/World Golf Hall of Fame.

DONALD ROSS

○ ○ ○

LIKE MANY OF HIS COUNTRYMEN, Donald Ross emigrated from Scotland to the United States around the turn of the century to become a golf professional. His true talent, however, proved to be designing golf courses. Incredibly, Ross would design or improve more than 500 courses during a 45-year career spent mainly on the western side of the Atlantic.

Ross was born in 1873 in Dornoch, Scotland, home of the Royal Dornoch links that would influence his own style as an architect. The son of a stonemason, he worked as an apprentice under the legendary Old Tom Morris in St. Andrews, then became pro and greenkeeper at Royal Dornoch. He was influenced to come to America by Robert Wilson, a Harvard professor who spent summers in Dornoch.

Ross arrived in the U.S. in 1898 with, it is said, two dollars in his pocket. That would soon change, thanks to his unique vision and ability to craft championship golf courses from all varieties of terrain, and his uncanny sense of how to improve existing ones. Wilson helped him land a job as pro at Oakley Country Club in Watertown, Massachusetts. Ross got an even bigger break shortly thereafter when he met James W. Tufts, whose family was building a new resort in Pinehurst, North Carolina. Ross signed on as the professional and quickly set about revising the first course there and designing a second one.

The Pinehurst No. 2 course, which would become his masterpiece, opened in 1903, and Ross continued to make changes on it until 1935. Ross's work at Pinehurst gained him a reputation as an architect, and his services were soon in demand as golf courses were sprouting up around the nation. By the 1920s, the golden age of architecture in the U.S., his company was working on dozens of projects at a time. Ross designed courses in 30 states, plus Canada and Cuba, though he remained affiliated with Pinehurst until his death in 1948. Ross's other famous courses include Seminole in Florida, Oakland Hills in Michigan, Oak Hill in New York, and Scioto and Inverness in Ohio. He is known for his natural use of the terrain and for crowned greens that offer subtle challenges on approach and pitch shots.

CAREER HIGHLIGHTS

Achievements: Won 1903, 1905, and 1906 North and South Opens at Pinehurst Country Club, where he served as pro. Revised first Pinehurst course and designed famed Pinehurst No. 2. Also designed Seminole (Florida), Oakland Hills (Michigan), Oak Hill (New York), Scioto (Ohio), and Inverness (Ohio). Designed or improved more than 500 courses.

PAUL RUNYAN

○ ○ ○

STANDING JUST 5'8 9/9 and weighing about 125 pounds, Paul Runyan was known as "Little Poison" because of his deadly game on and around the greens. His short-game skills earned him a pair of PGA Championships and a total of 29 victories, most of them in the 1930s.

The son of an Arkansas farmer, Runyan did not consider himself a natural as a player, but through hard work he reached the point where he was ready to try the pro tour in 1930 at the age of 21. Runyan won twice that year and scored at least one victory in every year of the 1930s except for 1937. He was the best player in the game for a two-year stretch, winning nine tournaments in 1933 and seven in 1934 and leading the money list both years. He played for the U.S. Ryder Cup team in 1933 and 1935.

Both of Runyan's PGA Championship victories came in final matches against long hitters. In 1934, he beat Craig Wood in a tense 38-hole match by getting up and down on the last three holes at Park Country Club in Williamsville, New York. At the 36th hole, both players made 12-foot par putts. Wood reached the par-5 37th hole in two, but Runyan was able to chip close for a tying birdie. Finally, Runyan claimed the match on the

38th hole by pitching over a bunker to eight feet and sinking the winning par putt.

Runyan's 1938 win over Sam Snead at Shawnee Country Club was an 8 & 7 romp, the biggest margin of victory in a final in the 39 years the PGA Championship was held at match play. Snead outdrove him by 50 yards on nearly every hole, but Runyan was deadly accurate the whole time and played the 29 holes of the final in 6-under.

Though Runyan was only 30 years old when he beat Snead, he added only two more victories, the last in 1941, and virtually retired from competition after World War II. Runyan went on to become a respected teacher, most notably for players having trouble with their putting, and a good senior player in the days before there was a Senior Tour, finishing second in the PGA Seniors Championship in 1959 and '60 and winning it in '61 and '62. He beat Sam King for the World Series title in each of those last two years.

Career Highlights
PGA Tour Victories: 29
Achievements: Won 1934 and 1938 PGA Championships; 1961 and 1962 PGA Seniors Championships. Led Tour in earnings in 1933 and 1934, winning 16 events over that two-year span. Recorded four top-four Masters finishes. Member of PGA/World Golf Hall of Fame.

DOUG SANDERS

○ ○ ○

WHILE HE IS REMEMBERED mostly for his flashy attire and for having the shortest backswing of any notable professional, Sanders was in fact an outstanding player. He ranks as one of the best players who never won a major, finishing with 20 wins in his PGA Tour career.

Sanders's closest brush with a major victory came in the 1970 British Open. Leading by one stroke with one hole remaining at the Old Course in St. Andrews, Scotland, Sanders misplayed a pitch shot to the short par-four 18th, left his first putt three feet short, and missed from there to fall into an 18-hole playoff with Jack Nicklaus. Sanders birdied the 18th the next day, but so did Nicklaus to win by one stroke.

Sanders had three other runner-up finishes in the majors. He tied for second behind Bob Rosburg in the 1959 PGA Championship, led the 1961 U.S. Open with nine holes to play before losing to Gene Littler, and tied for second behind Nicklaus in the 1966 British Open. On each occasion, Sanders was one stroke behind the winner. He also finished third in the 1960 and '61 PGA Championships and fourth in the 1972 British Open.

Sanders learned the game as a caddie at his hometown course in Cedartown, Georgia, and said he developed his short backswing because he wanted to stay in the fairway and not lose any of his small supply of balls. In 1956, Sanders became the first amateur to win the Canadian Open. In fact, no other amateur has ever captured the Canadian. He turned pro later in the year and went on to enjoy a lucrative career.

Sanders ranked in the top 10 money winners six times from 1960 to '67—10th in 1960, third in '61, seventh in '62, fourth in '65, fourth in '66, and sixth in '67. He had five victories in 1961 and three each in 1962 and '66.

It wasn't just his play that got Sanders noticed. He was one of the Tour's most notorious late-night partiers and big spenders, and certainly its most colorful dresser. Sanders often strode the fairways in such colors as canary yellow or mauve, with shoes to match.

CAREER HIGHLIGHTS
Earnings: $772,334
PGA Tour Victories: 20
Achievements: Won 1956 Canadian Open; 1958 Western Open; 1966 Bob Hope Desert Classic. Finished second in 1966 and 1970 British Opens; 1961 U.S. Open; 1959 PGA Championship. Is the only amateur ever to win Canadian Open. Won five Tour events in 1961.

Gene Sarazen

○ ○ ○

A FIRST-GENERATION AMERICAN and son of an immigrant Italian carpenter, Gene Sarazen, née Saraceni, was born in 1902 in Harrison, New York. Like all would-be golfers of the working class at that time, Sarazen got into golf as a caddie, at the age of 10.

"I walked to the course where I caddied (Apawamis G.C.) and made up nine holes along the way in empty lots," he said. He played them on the way to the course, and on the way home. "But nobody gave me lessons," he said. "I used to watch the players in tournaments. My favorite was Walter Hagen. I admired his ways, his technique, the way he would slash at the ball. And the way he dressed. He was my hero."

At 14, Sarazen came down with empyema, a lung ailment, and nearly died. "I remember lying in the hospital and the priests coming in and pulling the curtain around me," he said. "They figured I was going to go, and were preparing the last rites. That was in 1916, and in 1920 I was still so weak I could hardly break 80."

Two years later, he won the New Orleans Open, his first professional victory, and then surprised everyone (but himself) by becoming the winner of the U.S. Open. He won the '22 Open with the kind of verve, nerve, and brass that characterized his personality and golf game for the next 30 years. Four shots off the lead with one round to play at the Skokie Country Club, he caught fire. On the last hole, he was deep in contention and had a crucial decision to make.

"I hit a good drive," he said, "and for my second there was water to the left and out-of-bounds on the right. My caddie wanted me to play safe, but I heard somebody say [Bobby] Jones and [Bill] Mehlhorn [playing a few holes back] were doing well. So I said, 'Oh hell, give me that brassie.' I shot right for the green and put it about 12 feet from the cup. I made the putt for a birdie. On the 17th, Jones hit it out of bounds, and I won by a stroke."

Having taught himself to play golf, Sarazen gripped the club in an unorthodox manner that would have spelled disaster for average golfers off the tee.

He won with a 68, which tied the lowest final-round score ever made in the Open. Later in 1922, Sarazen won the PGA Championship. Two majors for a 20-year-old? Sarazen was indeed on his way. The next year, he successfully defended the PGA crown with a victory in the finals over his hero, Hagen.

At that time, the infant American pro tournament circuit offered very small purses, and Sarazen, who like Hagen was not interested in holding down a club job, made most of his income playing exhibitions. He put on a good show with his compact but powerful swing, and he was otherwise an innovative man who always found ways to promote himself and improve his game. He got much press when he insured his hands for well over $100,000. Putting poorly, he campaigned for a bigger hole—eight inches in diameter instead of 4¼. It was tried. It only made the good putters better, but Sarazen got plenty of "ink" for his idea. He would have another, more legitimate idea that everyone would adopt.

Like everyone of his generation, Sarazen was a poor sand bunker player because of the thin-bladed niblick (9-iron) that was used. Looking for an edge, Sarazen devised an angled flange for the back of the niblick so the club wouldn't dig into the sand so sharply. It was the first "sand wedge," as we have come to know it. Sarazen used it for the first time to capture the 1932 British Open. The club was revolutionary in its impact on the playing of golf.

Sarazen won 38 tournaments in his time, 22 of them from 1925 to '31, and is one of only four players in history to win all four major championships. He managed to keep his game intact through 1940, when he lost in a playoff to Lawson Little for the U.S. Open, but after 1941 he was never again a contender. However, he always had a knack for the spectacular. On the par-5 15th hole in the last round of the 1935 Masters, Sarazen holed his 4-wood second shot. The double eagle got him into a tie with Craig Wood, and Sarazen wound up the victor. The spectacular shot is often credited with getting the Masters on its way as a major championship.

In 1960, Sarazen was "rescued" from the obscurity of the record books when he was signed to host a television series, *Shell's Wonderful World of Golf*, which was extremely popular and ran for 10 years on network television. It stimulated even more interest in the game and made everyone once again conscious of Gene Sarazen. But just to make sure, in making a farewell appearance in the 1973 British Open at the age of 71, Sarazen made a hole-in-one on the famed "Postage Stamp" par-3 at Royal Troon. The next day, with the television cameras now following his every move, Sarazen holed a dramatic bunker shot for a birdie on the very same hole. Sarazen went out with a flair, just as he had come in.

CAREER HIGHLIGHTS
PGA Tour Victories: 38
Achievements: Won 1922 and 1932 U.S. Opens; 1922, 1923, and 1933 PGA Championships; 1935 Masters; 1932 British Open. At 20, became youngest U.S. Open winner. Member of PGA/World Golf Hall of Fame. Revolutionized golf with invention of the sand wedge. Hosted and made popular the 1960s TV show, *Shell's Wonderful World of Golf*.

Patty Sheehan

○ ○ ○

OF THE LPGA'S TOP PLAYERS in the 1980s and '90s, Patty Sheehan has been the most consistent performer. Starting in her first full season on the LPGA Tour, 1981, Sheehan won at least one tournament in every year except one through 1996. And she finished in the top 10 on the money list for 12 straight years, 1982–93.

Sheehan, who was born in Vermont and later moved to Nevada, was one of the top junior skiers in the country at age 13. She began to focus on golf, however, and won the first of four consecutive Nevada Amateurs at age 18 in 1975. She also won the California Amateur in 1978 and '79 and the national collegiate championship in 1980 while golfing for San Jose State. She was runner-up in the U.S. Women's Amateur in 1979.

Sheehan owns six titles in the three most important championships in women's golf, having captured three LPGA Championships (1983, '84, '93), two U.S. Women's Opens (1992, '94), and one Nabisco Dinah Shore (1996). She joined Mickey Wright (1960, '61) as the only back-to-back winners of the LPGA Championship, and Sheehan set the 18-hole tournament record with a 63 in 1984. Her most satisfying victories were the two Women's Opens, which came after finishing second in that event in 1983, '88, and '90. She lost a six-stroke lead after two rounds in 1990, but two years later she birdied the last two holes of regulation and then won a playoff against Juli Inkster for the title.

Sheehan is considered to have one of the most natural swings in women's golf, which has helped her to avoid slumps. Though she has never led the money list, she has ranked second in earnings five times (1983, '84, '88, '90, and '93), was the Player of the Year in 1983, and won the Vare Trophy for low scoring average in 1984. Multiple wins in 10 seasons helped her to 35 career victories through 1997. She also has been a regular on the U.S. Solheim Cup team.

Sheehan's highest victory total, five, came in 1990, the year after her northern California home was destroyed by an earthquake. She later built a new home in Reno, Nevada.

CAREER HIGHLIGHTS

Earnings: $5,130,937
LPGA Tour Victories: 35
Achievements: Won 1983, 1984, and 1993 LPGA Championships; 1992 and 1994 U.S. Women's Opens; 1996 Nabisco Dinah Shore. Tour Player of the Year in 1983. Vare Trophy winner in 1984. Four-time U.S. Solheim Cup team member. Member of LPGA Hall of Fame.

DENNY SHUTE

○ ○ ○

He didn't play the Tour as much as some of his contemporaries in the 1930s, devoting much time to his club job, but you could always count on Denny Shute to be a factor in the game's biggest events. Shute won back-to-back PGA Championships in 1936 and '37 (the last player to accomplish that feat), won the 1933 British Open, and had four finishes in the top four in the U.S. Open. He finished his career with 15 total victories.

Herman Densmore Shute, born in Cleveland in 1904, turned professional in 1928. He finished third in the 1929 U.S. Open and scored his first Tour win the same year. He won three tournaments in 1930, launching him to the first of three Ryder Cup appearances (1931, '33, and '37). His lowest moment came in the 1933 Ryder Cup at Southport, England, where he three-putted the last green to lose the decisive point to Syd Easterbrook. Two weeks later, however, Shute won the British Open at St. Andrews. Four straight rounds of 73 got him into a 36-hole playoff with fellow American Craig Wood, and Shute prevailed, 149 to 154.

Shute finished second in the 1931 PGA Championship, losing to Tom Creavy in the final, and reached the semifinals in 1934. His two-year championship run started in 1936, when he nipped Bill Mehlhorn, 1 up, in the semifinals, and went against long-hitting Jimmy Thomson in the final at Pinehurst. For most of the match, Shute's superior putting was the difference, then he finished in spectacular fashion with an eagle on the 34th hole. Shute received some help from Harold McSpaden in the 1937 final at the Pittsburgh Field Club. Two down with three holes to play, Shute won the 34th and 35th holes with a par and a bogey, then watched McSpaden miss a four-foot birdie putt on the 36th. Shute won with a par on the 37th hole.

Shute nearly added a pair of U.S. Opens, but settled for second place in both: in 1939, when he tied Craig Wood and Byron Nelson before Nelson won the playoff, and in 1941, when he finished three behind Wood. Shute was not a regular on the early Tour, and he did not compete much at all after World War II. His success is stunning when one considers how little he played.

CAREER HIGHLIGHTS
PGA Tour Victories: 15
Achievements: Won 1933 British Open; 1936 and 1937 PGA Championships. Registered five top-six finishes in the U.S. Open. Fired four rounds of 73 at St. Andrews and won playoff against Craig Wood in 1933 British Open for his first major championship. Competed on U.S. Ryder Cup teams in 1931, 1933, and 1937.

CHARLES SIFFORD

○ ○ ○

THE FIRST AFRICAN AMERICAN to play regularly on the PGA Tour, Charles Sifford endured many hardships before scoring a pair of victories in the late 1960s after he was in his 40s. Sifford can be considered golf's Jackie Robinson, but the process of integration was a much slower one in golf than it was in baseball.

Sifford was born in Charlotte, North Carolina, in 1923. He learned to play golf in the only way then available to an African American—as a caddie. After serving in the army and moving north, Sifford got a break of sorts when he became the private golf professional for singer Billy Eckstine in the late 1940s. Sifford, along with Ted Rhodes and a couple of other black golfers, clearly had the talent to play the PGA Tour. However, there were only a couple of events that would let them play during the early 1950s (the U.S. Open and Los Angeles Open).

There was not one defining moment when pro golf became integrated. It was up to each tournament whether it would allow black players, and through the 1950s only a few more events opened the gates. In fact, the PGA itself had a Caucasianonly clause that prevented blacks from being members. This didn't fall until 1960, when it was challenged by the State of California.

Meanwhile, Sifford managed to win the 1957 Long Beach Open, which had too small a purse to be considered an official event, and the Negro National Open six times, as he tried to scratch out a living. Finally, by the early 1960s, virtually the entire Tour opened up to blacks, but that meant some difficult trips through the South, where Sifford had to endure racial taunts and often was not allowed into all parts of the clubhouse. It will never be known what Sifford could have accomplished if he had been able to play the Tour full-time in his prime. Fortunately, he remained competitive into his 40s, and he captured the 1967 Hartford Open at age 43, becoming the first African American to win on the PGA Tour. He also won the 1969 Los Angeles Open. Tiger Woods is among those who credits Sifford for opening golf's doors to minorities.

CAREER HIGHLIGHTS

Earnings: $339,960 (PGA); $927,790 (SR)
Tour Victories: 2 (PGA); 2 (SR)
Achievements: Won 1967 Hartford Open; 1969 Los Angeles Open. Became first black to win Tour event in 1967 Hartford Open. Captured six Negro National Open titles. Became first black winner of PGA Seniors Championship in 1975. Ranked among top 60 in Tour earnings from 1960 to 1969.

HORTON SMITH

○ ○ ○

NO PLAYER IN THE HISTORY of the pro Tour has gotten off to a faster start in his career than Horton Smith. The lanky Missourian came on the scene in 1928 and won a startling eight events during the 1928–29 winter tour when he was just 20 years old. He couldn't continue at that pace—indeed, no one ever has—but Smith went on to have a very good career, finishing with 31 victories and winning two of the first three Masters.

Smith was one of the best putters of his time, and he had a smooth swing—though some wondered why he always seemed to be experimenting with it. Perhaps he was trying to recapture the magic of 1928–29. His first two wins came late in 1928, and he scored a Tour-high eight wins in 1929 (six early in the year and two late). Four more victories followed in 1930 before Smith hit a bit of a drought, winning just once in each of the next three years.

In 1934, Smith captured the inaugural Masters, getting a birdie on the 71st hole and finishing one stroke ahead of Craig Wood. He won the tournament in similar fashion in 1936, taking the lead on the next-to-last hole and beating Harry Cooper by one. Smith never captured the U.S. Open, finishing third in 1930 and 1940 after taking at least a share of the lead into the 36-hole final day each time. He also was third in the 1930 British Open.

Few have enjoyed as much success in Ryder Cup play as Smith. Competing for the U.S. in the 1929, '33, and '35 Matches, he never lost. Smith was also chosen for the 1939 and '41 Matches, which were not played due to the war.

Smith won two or three events each year from 1934 through '37, but he managed only two more wins after turning 30, both of them in 1941. He played the PGA Tour very little after World War II. Smith had become involved in Tournament administration early in his career, becoming a member of the Tournament committee as early as 1933. He served as president of the PGA from 1952 to '54. Smith is perhaps the first player to have used a club specifically designed for hitting the ball out of the sand, but the concave-face model he used was later banned.

CAREER HIGHLIGHTS
PGA Tour Victories: 31
Achievements: Won 1934 and 1936 Masters. Posted top-three finishes in the U.S. Open and British Open in the 1930s. Won eight Tour events in 1929. Led Tour in earnings in 1936. Served as PGA president from 1952 to 1954. Member of PGA/World Golf Hall of Fame.

Macdonald Smith

○ ○ ○

His brothers Alex and Willie both won the U.S. Open, but Macdonald Smith was undoubtedly the best of the three though his record in the U.S. and British Opens was one of frustration. Smith never won either national title despite finishing second four times (two each in the U.S. and the British) and in the top six 14 times. He came within three strokes of the winner on 10 occasions.

Smith was more successful in other tournaments. The PGA Tour, which begins its records in 1916, credits him with 24 official wins, but he also won seven earlier tournaments. He would have won more if he hadn't left the game for six years, going to work in a shipyard during World War I and not returning until 1923. Thought to have one of the game's best swings, Smith enjoyed a long career, even with the hiatus. His last victory, at age 46 in 1936, came 26 years after his first.

Smith, like his older brothers, was born in Carnoustie, Scotland, but all emigrated to America to become golf pros. Macdonald won three tournaments in 1910 and also got into a playoff in the U.S. Open that year with his brother Alex—the eventual winner—and John McDermott. For the rest of his career in national opens, Macdonald always seemed to produce a great final round when he was too far back to win or a poor final round when he was in good position. These were not habits conducive to wining major championships, and thus Smith struggled to do so.

His best chance came in the 1925 British Open at Prestwick, Scotland. Smith took a five-stroke lead into the final round, but he lost his composure due to a huge, swarming gallery and poor crowd control and finished with an 82. A mere 76 would have given Smith the championship. He was runner-up to Bobby Jones in both the U.S. and British Opens in 1930 and also second in the 1932 British Open.

Smith did win some significant events during his career, including three Western Opens and four Los Angeles Opens. Between 1924 and '36 he won at least one tournament in all but one year, including five victories in 1926.

CAREER HIGHLIGHTS
PGA Tour Victories: 24
Achievements: Won 1912, 1925, and 1933 Western Opens; 1928, 1929, 1932, and 1934 Los Angeles Opens. Finished within three shots of the winner in 12 U.S. or British Opens between 1910 and 1935, including two runner-up finishes in each. Won five Tour events in 1926.

SAM SNEAD

○ ○ ○

AN IMAGE OF THE GOLF SWING that Sam Snead liked to project was: "It should feel oily." He spoke from personal experience, for Snead had one of the smoothest swings the game of golf has ever known.

So fluid and full was Snead's swing, people thought he was double-jointed. Snead always smiled at the remark, enjoyed the compliment, but noted, "No one has double joints. I'm just loose-jointed. That's the proper way to put it." In fact, he was born with his vertebrae out of line. "I'd have been two inches taller if not for that," he said. Snead could have gone to college on an athletic scholarship in baseball or football, but his high school coach advised Sam that if he spent the four years in golf rather than in college, he would be further ahead. "I wanted to be an athlete," said Sam, and that he was.

His natural talent was monumental, and despite the misaligned vertebrae he was an amazing physical specimen who maintained his highest level of play for an uncommonly long period of time. Snead won his first tournament as a professional in 1936. He won his last on the regular PGA Tour, the Greater Greensboro Open, in 1965, when he was just short of his 53rd birthday. That made him the oldest winner ever on the Tour, a record that might well be etched in stone.

Samuel Jackson Snead was born in Hot Springs, Virginia, in 1912. He began caddying and playing golf at age seven at the famed Homestead Hotel, where his father worked as a maintenance engineer. A marvelous storyteller, Snead once recalled in *Gettin' to the Dance Floor: An Oral History of American Golf* his first days at golf:

"My uncle used to come up on Sunday and get me by the hair and say, 'Come on, let's go pitch horseshoes....' He couldn't beat me. So one day I was out back fooling around chipping—see, I put some tomato cans in the ground to make some holes and I'd chip with a jigger, which was like a 5-iron—and my uncle said, 'Gimme that,' meaning the jigger. So now we stopped playing horseshoes and started chipping. I beat him at that, too. Then one Sunday he came up with a bag of clubs, half left-handed, half right-handed, and said, 'C'mon, damn you, we're going up to the Goat.' That was the name of the little nine-hole course at the hotel where we could play. You'd play six holes up the mountain, and three of them off it. After a hole I'd ask my uncle, 'What'd you have, Uncle Ed?' He'd say he had a 5 or 4 and I'd say, 'Yeah, but you whiffed it down there a couple of times,' and he said, 'Son, those were practice swings,' and I said, 'No, you grunted. When you grunt, you made an effort and it counts.'"

"That was my first golf, up and down the Goat. Oh, they wouldn't allow us on the regular courses—Cascades, Upper Cascades—but we'd slip on through a wooded area at the far end where a green was and chip and putt. If we saw somebody, we'd head for the brush."

"Show me a golfer who walks away calmly after topping a drive or missing a kick-in putt, and I'll show you one who is going to lose."
—SAM SNEAD

It wasn't too long before Snead would be welcome at every great and famous golf course in the world. He started as a professional making clubs in the Homestead pro shop, also gave a few lessons, and then at age 20 was made the pro at the Cascades course. It was there that he began developing, or perfecting, his remarkably graceful swing and honing his championship game. "There hadn't been a pro there since the Crash of '29," Snead recalled. "So I had a chance to practice, and I beat sod. Oh, I beat sod. They said, 'Hey, you're beatin' all the grass off.' I broke the course record twice the first two weeks on the job."

Snead played on the PGA Tour for the first time in the 1935 Miami Open, making the trip in a Model A Ford. It took 2½ days to get there. "Going down through Georgia," Snead remembered, "there were one-way wooden bridges that might be 300 yards long and you had to look ahead to see if there was anyone at the other end coming on. If he was on first, then you'd have to wait your turn to get over." Two years later, Snead put together enough money to travel to California for the West Coast portion of the winter tour, and it was then that Snead's playing career, and public persona, emerged.

Snead won $600 in the Los Angeles Open. The next week, he won the Oakland Open, from which an anecdote was born that became the yardstick by which Snead's personality was measured for all time. His picture appeared in *The New York Times*, and upon seeing it Snead asked Tour manager Fred Corcoran how his picture got in a New York newspaper when he'd never been in that city. Corcoran, a master promoter of the Tour who knew a good line when he heard one—and who became Snead's business manager—never tired of relating that story. It brought attention to the circuit and established Snead as a kind of naive mountain boy. It worked, largely because Snead became one of the greatest players in the history of the game.

Snead won four more times in 1937, and the next year he won eight events on the circuit, a record total that would not be topped until 1945. In '37, it appeared Snead would also win the U.S. Open. He shot a final-round 71 at Oakland Hills Country Club, but a late rush by Ralph Guldahl (69) put Snead second by two strokes. It was the beginning of Snead's career-long disappointment in the national championship. He would win an official 81 tournaments on the PGA Tour, including three Masters and three PGA Championships—plus one British Open—yet he would never win the U.S. Open. He came close a number of times, including a playoff loss to Lew Worsham in 1947.

It was said that Snead lost his nerve for the most coveted of championships in 1939 by taking an 8 on the last hole when a 5 (par) would have brought him victory. Some would also suggest that because Snead never won the U.S. Open, he was not the complete champion that his archrival, four-time U.S. Open winner Ben Hogan, was. And yet, in the three times Snead was in a playoff head-to-head against Hogan—including once for the Masters—he won every time.

Of the many comments Snead would make when asked about his U.S. Open record, the most incisive was: "When they say that I couldn't win the big one, I ask: What do you call all those others? What's big and what's small?" Indeed, Snead's seven triumphs in the modern majors is a number surpassed by only five other golfers. In 1946, he proved he could win in the granddaddy of tournaments, the British Open, on the grandest course, St. Andrews. He prevailed by a full four strokes.

Because of his incredible longevity as a first-class golfer, Snead was on the ground floor of, and a significant factor in, the development and growth of the Senior PGA Tour. In the first Legends of Golf event, the tournament that gave rise to the Senior circuit, Snead—on national television—put on a display of birdie golf on the final nine to bring him and his partner, Gardner Dickinson, an extremely popular and wonder-filled victory. At the age of 66, and by now finally retired from PGA Tour golf, Snead's swing was just as oily as ever as he outdrove and outplayed two golfers 17 years his junior—Peter Thomson and Kel Nagle—to win by a stroke.

Indeed, as a senior golfer before the Senior PGA Tour began to blossom, Snead won six PGA Seniors Championships, five World Seniors, and—in 1982 with Don January—yet another Legends of Golf tournament. And he never grunted. Not once.

CAREER HIGHLIGHTS

Earnings: $620,126
PGA Tour Victories: 81
Achievements: Won 1942, 1949, and 1951 PGA Championships; 1949, 1952, and 1954 Masters; 1946 British Open. Won Greater Greensboro Open eight times from 1938 to 1965. Led Tour in earnings in 1938, 1949, and 1950. Vardon Trophy winner in 1938, 1949, 1950, and 1955. PGA Player of the Year in 1949. Member of PGA/World Golf Hall of Fame. Captured 11 Tour events in 1950. Earned money in 42 of 44 years on Tour.

JAN STEPHENSON

○ ○ ○

During the 1970s and '80s, Australia's Jan Stephenson became not only one of the LPGA Tour's first sex symbols, but also one of its leading players. Included in her 16 career victories are three of the four modern major championships: the Peter Jackson Classic (now the du Maurier), the LPGA Championship, and the U.S. Women's Open. She lacks only the Nabisco Dinah Shore for a career Grand Slam.

After an outstanding amateur career and one year of dominating the small Australian women's tour, Stephenson headed for the United States in 1974 at age 22. She made an immediate impact, both with her play (never worse than 34th on the money list in her first 15 years on Tour) and her looks. Throughout the 1970s and through the mid-1980s, Stephenson posed on calendars and posters and created controversy among some of her fellow pros for what they considered risqué poses in the LPGA's *Fairway Magazine*.

Stephenson's first two LPGA victories came in 1976, with one more each in 1978 and '80 before Stephenson hit her best years. All three of her majors came in tight battles against outstanding players. She beat Nancy Lopez and Pat Bradley by one stroke in the 1981 Peter Jackson Classic, Jo Anne Carner by two strokes in the 1982 LPGA Championship, and Carner and Patty Sheehan by one stroke in the 1983 U.S. Women's Open. She also came close to winning the Nabisco Dinah Shore, finishing second in 1985.

Stephenson, who was the first from the LPGA Tour ranks to become a golf course designer, set a record scoring total for a 54-hole event (since broken) when she shot a 198 to win the 1981 Mary Kay Classic by 11 strokes. She finished among the top 15 money winners in every year but one from 1976 to '88. Starting in the mid-1980s, Stephenson began to complain of poor putting. She has also had more than her share of misfortune, including a 1987 car accident after which she was able to forge a comeback (scoring her last three career victories late in the year) and a 1990 mugging which left her with a broken finger from which she never fully recovered.

CAREER HIGHLIGHTS
Earnings: $2,427,142
LPGA Tour Victories: 16
Achievements: Won 1981 Peter Jackson Classic; 1982 LPGA Championship; 1983 U.S. Women's Open. LPGA Rookie of the Year in 1974. Totaled 16 top-10 and 10 top-five finishes in 1988, earning $236,739. Has won 15 events internationally. Became first LPGA pro to design golf courses.

CURTIS STRANGE

○ ○ ○

ONLY SIX PLAYERS HAVE EVER WON back-to-back U.S. Open championships, and the only one to do so in the last 40 years is Curtis Strange. When he accomplished the feat in 1988–89, it was the signal achievement of a five-year span during which Strange won 12 tournaments and led the money list three times.

Strange's father, Tom, was a Virginia club professional who had played in the U.S. Open. He died when Curtis was 14. Strange built an outstanding amateur record, with his most impressive victory coming as a freshman at Wake Forest in the 1974 NCAA Championship. He eagled the final hole there to earn both the individual and team titles. Strange also won the 1973 Southeastern Amateur, the 1974 Western Amateur, the 1975 Eastern Amateur, and the 1975 and '76 North and South Amateurs. A long hitter in his amateur days, Strange throttled back when he turned pro in order to gain more control.

Strange left college in his junior year to turn pro in 1976, but he didn't score his first Tour win until the last event of 1979. He blossomed in 1985, when he won three times and led the money list. Strange's finest seasons came in 1987 and '88, when he led the Tour in earnings each year, totaling more than $2 million.

Going into the 1988 U.S. Open, Strange had done nearly everything except win a major championship. He finally claimed his first major at The Country Club, getting up-and-down from a bunker on the 72nd hole and then defeating Nick Faldo in a playoff. Strange defended the U.S. Open title the next year, passing a faltering Tom Kite on the final day at Oak Hill with a round that included 16 pars, one birdie, and one bogey.

Strange challenged for a third straight Open title in 1990 before dropping back in the final round. He later admitted he lost his motivation for the next couple of years, and he also had physical problems. His drive to compete and his health later returned, but his game didn't make it all the way back. He remained winless in the 1990s through 1997.

CAREER HIGHLIGHTS
Earnings: $6,973,501
PGA Tour Victories: 17
Achievements: Won 1988 and 1989 U.S. Opens; 1985 and 1987 Canadian Opens; 1974 NCAA Championship. First to successfully defend U.S. Open title since Ben Hogan in 1951. First to earn $1 million in a single season in 1988. Also led Tour in earnings in 1985 and 1987. Tour Player of the Year in 1988.

LOUISE SUGGS

○ ○ ○

IN THE EARLY DAYS OF THE LPGA Tour, Louise Suggs said that watching herself, Patty Berg, and Babe Zaharias compete for tournament titles was like "watching three cats fight over a plate of fish." Suggs, a founding member of the LPGA, won her share, compiling 50 victories from 1949 through 1962 to rank fifth on the all-time list.

Suggs was capable of some of the lowest scoring of her era. She shot a 291 total to win the 1949 U.S. Women's Open title by 14 strokes, still an LPGA record for victory margin. She won a second U.S. Open, in 1952, by seven strokes with a 284 total, albeit on a 5,460-yard, par-69 course in Philadelphia.

Suggs, born in Atlanta in 1923, learned the game from her father at age 10 and won the Georgia Amateur when she was 16. She was an outstanding amateur, winning the North and South Amateur three times, sweeping the Western Amateur and Western Open in both 1946 and '47, and taking the Titleholders in 1946. Then came victories in the biggest amateur events on either side of the Atlantic, the U.S. Amateur in 1947 and the British championship in 1948. Suggs turned pro in the summer of 1948 rather than defend her U.S. Amateur title. But the Women's Professional Golf

Association was foundering, and the next year Suggs became a charter member of the LPGA.

In addition to her two U.S. Women's Opens, Suggs won three Titleholders (1954, '55, and '59), two Western Opens (1949, '53), and one LPGA Championship (1957) for a total of eight major championships as a pro. She also was runner-up in five Women's Opens and four LPGA Championships. Her best stretch came in 1952, '53, and '54 when she won six, eight, and five tournaments. Suggs led the money list in 1953 and '60 and earned the Vare Trophy for low scoring average in 1957. In 1951, she became the first inductee to the LPGA Hall of Fame.

Suggs cut back her schedule after 1961, but as late as 1963, at age 39, she was second in both the U.S. Women's Open and LPGA Championship. She eventually served as LPGA president three times.

CAREER HIGHLIGHTS

Earnings: $190,475 (due to loss of early LPGA records, this falls short of her actual earnings)

LPGA Tour Victories: 50

Achievements: Won 1949 and 1952 U.S. Women's Opens; 1949 and 1953 Western Opens; 1954, 1956, and 1959 Titleholders Championships; 1957 LPGA Championship. Led Tour in earnings in 1953 and 1960. Vare Trophy winner in 1957. Founder and charter member of LPGA. Member of PGA/World Golf Hall of Fame and LPGA Hall of Fame.

JOHN H. TAYLOR

○ ○ ○

THE BRITISH ARMY AND NAVY rejected John H. Taylor due to his poor eyesight, but their loss proved to be golf's gain. Taylor won five British Opens from 1894 through 1913, joining Harry Vardon and James Braid as part of the Great Triumvirate. His swing wasn't as graceful as Vardon's or as powerful as Braid's, but Taylor was considered the best putter of the three and was an excellent foul-weather player. He holds the British Open record for top-10 finishes with 23, including 17 in a row.

Taylor was born in England in 1871. He quit school at age 11 and worked at various jobs before becoming a greenkeeper. He entered his first British Open in 1893 and led after one round, then fell back. He won the next year at Sandwich in the first Open held in England, becoming the first of the Triumvirate to claim the title, and he successfully defended in 1895 at St. Andrews. Taylor nearly made it three in a row, but he dropped a playoff to Vardon in 1896 at Muirfield. Taylor had led by three entering the final round.

Taylor won his third Open in 1900 in an eight-stroke romp at St. Andrews. That year, he made an exhibition tour of the United States with Vardon;

in his only U.S. Open appearance, Taylor finished second to his countryman. Taylor became familiar with the runner-up spot in the British Open, finishing second four times in a row starting in 1904. He shot a record 68 in the final round in 1904 but fell one stroke short of Jack White. Conversely, he lost the 54-hole lead in 1906 and 1907, settling for second place each time.

Taylor regained his winning touch in 1909, taking the Open by four strokes at Deal. His final title came in 1913 at Hoylake, when he won by eight in a driving storm. If he had played better in the final round in 1914, it would have been Taylor, not Vardon, with six Open championships. But Taylor faltered with a closing 83 as Vardon passed him. Taylor was the only one of the Triumvirate to contend in an Open after World War I, and he finished sixth as late as 1925 at age 54. Taylor was made an honorary member of the Royal & Ancient in 1949 and later served as president of the Royal North Devon Country Club.

CAREER HIGHLIGHTS

Achievements: Won 1894, 1895, 1900, 1909, and 1913 British Opens. Finished among British Open top 10 a record 23 times, including 17 in a row. Runner-up in 1900 U.S. Open. Played in first Great Britain-versus-USA match in 1921. Captained winning British Ryder Cup team in 1933. Member of PGA/World Golf Hall of Fame.

PETER THOMSON

○ ○ ○

Australia's Peter Thomson won only once in the United States, where he competed irregularly, but during the 1950s he reigned supreme in the British Open. Thomson finished with five British Open titles, a total surpassed by only Harry Vardon. His remarkable run included finishing first or second in seven consecutive years.

Thomson, born in 1929 in Melbourne, learned the game on his own as a teenager. His first tournament title came in the 1950 New Zealand Open. The next year, at age 21, he played in his first British Open and finished sixth. Then began his seven-year stretch of four wins and three seconds. Thomson was second in 1952 and '53, and he won three in a row beginning in 1954. He was the first to take three straight Opens since Robert Ferguson in the 19th century. After a runner-up finish in 1957, Thomson rebounded to take the 1958 title in a playoff over Dave Thomas.

Thomson won his fifth British Open in 1965, a satisfying victory because the top Americans were then making the trip to the British Open. That hadn't been the case in the 1950s, though international players Bobby Locke of South Africa

Roberto De Vicenzo of Argentina provided competition.

During the late 1950s, Thomson tried the U.S. circuit on occasion. His only victory came in the 1956 Texas International Open. He finished fourth in the 1956 U.S. Open after holding the 36-hole lead and was fifth in the 1957 Masters. Thomson never felt completely comfortable in the U.S. with its lush fairways; his low, running shots were better suited to links golf. Thomson won 26 events in Europe. He also captured nine New Zealand Opens and three Australian Opens.

With the birth of the Senior Tour in the 1980s, Thomson got a second chance in the U.S. He won 11 Senior tournaments, including the 1984 PGA Seniors Championship. His nine wins in 1985 set a Senior Tour record. Thomson, always a man with diverse interests (he once ran for the Victorian state senate), quit competing in the late 1980s while remaining active in course design and golf journalism.

CAREER HIGHLIGHTS

Achievements: Won 1954, 1955, 1956, 1958, and 1965 British Opens. Nine-time champion of New Zealand Open. First since "Young" Tom Morris to win three consecutive British Opens. Recorded top-five finishes in U.S. Open and Masters. Winner of more than 50 tournaments worldwide. Member of PGA/World Golf Hall of Fame.

JEROME TRAVERS

○ ○ ○

ONE OF THE GAME'S MOST ENIGMATIC champions, Jerome Travers is one of only two players to win at least four U.S. Amateur titles (Bobby Jones won five). Those victories came in 1907, '08, '12, and '13. Thought to excel only at match play, Travers pulled off a surprising victory in the 1915 U.S. Open, then retired from competition at the end of that year at age 28.

Travers was born on Long Island and came under the tutelage of Alex Smith at Nassau Country Club. He developed a rivalry with three-time U.S. Amateur champion Walter J. Travis, another Long Island resident. Travers, then 17, defeated the 42-year-old Travis in the 1904 Nassau Invitational. Travis knocked off Travers in the quarterfinal of the 1906 U.S. Amateur, but thereafter Travers had the edge on his older foe, beating him five times in the U.S. Amateur.

Travers's first two U.S. Amateur victories were romps in the finals, 6 & 5 over Archibald Graham in 1907 and 8 & 7 over Max Behr in 1908. Travers didn't enter the next two U.S. Amateurs. It is not known why, although it is possible that he chose to play only when he felt absolutely ready. He was known for his fierce desire to win, and it served him well in championship golf.

Travers returned in 1911, losing to eventual winner Harold Hilton, then won by large margins again in the next two years—7 & 6 over Chick Evans in 1912 and 5 & 4 over John Anderson in 1913. Travers lost in the final to Francis Ouimet in 1914.

Though he was one of the game's toughest competitors and owned an excellent short game, Travers was a wild driver and sometimes resorted to hitting irons off the tee. Before 1915, he had entered only three U.S. Opens, finishing no better than 25th in any of them. But that year at Baltusrol, he played the last six holes in 1-under to score a one-stroke victory over Tom McNamara. It was the last Open he played in. He didn't play in another U.S. Amateur either, saying it wasn't possible to both earn a living and play championship golf. He spent the last years of his life as an aircraft-engine inspector.

CAREER HIGHLIGHTS
Achievements: Won 1907, 1908, 1912, and 1913 U.S. Amateur Championships; 1915 U.S. Open. Only man other than Bobby Jones to win four U.S. Amateurs. One of five amateurs to win U.S. Open. Three-time winner of New Jersey Amateur and five-time winner of Metropolitan Amateur. Member of PGA/World Golf Hall of Fame.

Walter Travis

○ ○ ○

He didn't even play golf until he was 35 years old, but Walter Travis became one of the top figures in American golf at the start of the 20th century and was the first player from America to win the British Amateur.

Travis was actually born in Australia in 1862, but his family moved to the States when he was a boy. He didn't take up golf until 1897, but he caught on quickly—he reached the semifinals of the U.S. Amateur one year later. Travis also made the semifinals in 1899, then won the U.S. Amateur in 1900, '01, and '03. During that stretch, he won the qualifying medal in 1900, '01, and '02 (there was no qualifying in 1903).

Looking for another world to conquer, Travis decided to enter the 1904 British Amateur at Royal St. George's. He beat such top players as Harold Hilton and Horace Hutchinson on the way to the final, where he squared off against long-hitting Edward Blackwell. Travis was a short hitter, but he was deadly accurate and an outstanding putter. Those attributes carried him to a 4 & 3 victory. The win was not a popular one among his British hosts, who were put off by Travis's gruff manner.

Travis, for his part, felt he had been given an unfriendly welcome. A few months later, the center-shafted Schenectady putter used by Travis in his victory was banned in Britain, though not in America.

By then, Travis was in his 40s, and he didn't win any more U.S. Amateurs (or enter any more British Amateurs). But he remained remarkably competitive for another decade, taking the qualifying medal in the 1906, '07, and '08 U.S. Amateurs and reaching the semifinals in 1906, '08, and '14. He won the 1915 Metropolitan Amateur championship at the age of 53.

Travis also made contributions to the game in other areas. He founded *The American Golfer* magazine in 1908 and served as its editor for many years. He became involved in designing courses, including Garden City Golf Club on Long Island and Westchester Country Club just north of New York City. His amateur status was stripped in 1910 because of these endeavors but was later restored.

CAREER HIGHLIGHTS

Achievements: Won 1900, 1901, and 1903 U.S. Amateur Championships; 1904 British Amateur Championship. Became first overseas player to win British Amateur. Finished second in 1902 U.S. Open. Reached semifinals of U.S. Amateur eight times. Founded *The American Golfer* magazine. Member of PGA/World Golf Hall of Fame.

LEE TREVINO

○ ○ ○

LEE TREVINO'S FIRST EXPERIENCE in golf was as a preteen hunting golf balls hit out of bounds into a field near where he lived—a simple four-room wooden house with no electricity or plumbing. There was nowhere for him to go but up. He succeeded on the strength of an overwhelming desire to do just that. He made himself a man of means playing a game at which he worked very hard.

Born in 1939 in Dallas, Lee Buck Trevino was raised by his mother and a grandfather. He left school after the eighth grade to earn money for the family by working at a par-3 course. After serving four years as an enlistee in the Marine Corps, Trevino returned to work at the par-3 as well as at a driving range. But he made more money wagering on himself at golf—and not all of it the "traditional" kind. His most famous hustle was hitting his shots with the fat end of a taped-up Dr Pepper bottle and putting with the thin end, a la billiards.

As his game with real clubs improved, the bets got bigger and so did the competition. Once in the early 1960s, Raymond Floyd—already a nationally known golfer who also liked to play high-stakes golf off the PGA Tour—got hooked up in Texas against a fellow named Trevino. Floyd left lighter in his wallet, and he was glad to be free of the then-unknown Mexican-American with the tattoos who putted with the fine touch of a safecracker and had even more nerve. Of course, Floyd would not be free of Trevino, nor would any other Tour golfer.

In his formative years, Trevino had a "classic" swing, but it just didn't work. He hooked the ball badly under pressure. Then one day he watched from afar Ben Hogan practicing, and he liked the controlled left-to-right fade Hogan hit, one after another. Trevino decided that flight pattern was for him, and for five years, on his own, he worked on a way to accomplish it. In the end, it didn't look at all like Hogan's swing, if only because of Trevino's short, chunky physique, but he got the same result. And then some. No one questions the assessment that Trevino became the best ball-striker since Hogan. In the 1990s, he was once asked when he last hit a ball out of bounds. In all sincerity, he couldn't remember. Nor could anyone else.

"No one who ever had lessons would have a swing like mine," said Trevino.

Trevino turned professional in 1960, but he somehow never joined the PGA of America and thus did not qualify to play on the Tour, then run by that organization. He had to play in open events, and in 1965 he won the highly competitive Texas State Open. In his first U.S. Open, in 1966, he made the cut and finished 54th. He continued to practice, give some lessons at an El Paso club where he was an assistant pro, and hustle on the golf course to take care of a growing family by his first wife. It was she who suggested Trevino enter the 1967 U.S. Open, being played in New Jersey.

Trevino scraped together some money, lived inexpensively far from the course (Baltusrol Golf Course), and made his name known for the first time outside of Texas by finishing a very solid fifth in the championship. With the $6,000 he took in, and a showing that enabled him to get into subsequent Tour events that year, Trevino won another $20,000. He was set, financially and game-wise, to begin his invasion of major-league professional golf. He was indeed an overnight sensation.

At the 1968 U.S. Open, Trevino stayed close to the lead through three rounds, then canned two birdie putts at the 65th and 66th holes with a combined length of 55 feet to ice victory. He became the first ever to win a U.S. Open with all four rounds in the 60s. The brilliant golf, combined with a quick and funny wit delivered with the panache of a stand-up comic, turned Trevino into a gallery favorite.

From 1968 through '84 on the PGA Tour, Trevino won 27 times, including another U.S. Open (in a playoff with Jack Nicklaus) and two PGA Championships, the last coming at the age of 44. Not even lightning could stop him. Trevino (along with golfers Jerry Heard and Bobby Nichols) was struck by lightning during play in the 1975 Western Open. Still, at 36, he recovered enough to win nine more PGA Tour events, including his second PGA Championship (sixth major), and 26 Senior Tour events from 1990 to '95. Near the end of 1995, however, Trevino had major back surgery in which a permanent plate was inserted through his neck to fuse disks.

The back problem may have derived in part from the lightning bolt, but more likely it resulted from having hit hundreds of practice balls every day, day in and day out, for years. All the hard work had finally caught up with him, but by then the poor kid from the other side of the tracks had become a multimillionaire—and one of the most accomplished and popular golfers the game has ever seen.

CAREER HIGHLIGHTS

Earnings: $3,478,450 (PGA); $7,449,561 (SR)
Tour Victories: 27 (PGA); 27 (SR)
Achievements: Won 1968 and 1971 U.S. Opens; 1974 and 1984 PGA Championships; 1971 and 1972 British Opens; 1992 and 1994 PGA Seniors Championship; 1992 Tradition; 1990 U.S. Senior Open. First player in U.S. Open history to shoot all four rounds under par and in the 60s (1968). Five-time Vardon Trophy winner and 1971 Player of the Year. Member of PGA/World Golf Hall of Fame.

HARRY VARDON

○ ○ ○

In 1900, Harry Vardon, a 30-year-old Englishman born on the Isle of Jersey, played an extensive exhibition tour of the United States. It was meant to promote interest in what was still a very new game to the United States, and at the same time publicize a new golf ball, the Vardon Flyer, made by the A. G. Spalding Co. Vardon was chosen because he was the best golfer in the world. The year before, Vardon had won his third British Open (he would win six Opens, a record to this day).

The choice of Vardon served the purpose of inspiring people to take up the game because of his smooth and elegant swing. Vardon, who was sometimes referred to as "The Greyhound," is considered the "father of the modern golf swing." He was the first to make a science of the swing, working out mechanics that everyone could understand and try to emulate. He did not in fact invent the golf grip named after him—in which the little finger of the lower hand on the club overlaps the index finger of the opposite hand—but he is certainly responsible for its dissemination. The Vardon Grip, which Vardon said best unified the hands for a more consistent swing, is to this day used by the majority of the world's golfers. Vardon was also known for his accuracy, which he combined with considerable power, but it was the latter that his first American audiences admired most.

Vardon recalled in a book about his first trip to America: "At that period, the Americans were not sufficiently advanced [in golf] to appreciate the finer points of the game. They did, however, appear to thoroughly enjoy the type of ball I drove. I hit it high for carry, which resembled a home run."

"A golfer's swing is often made for good or bad in the first week of his experience."
—HARRY VARDON

For his 1900 tour of the United States, Vardon traveled over 20,000 miles, going as far west as Chicago and throughout the Southeastern states. Except for a break to return home to defend his British Open title (he finished second), his 1900 tour extended through most of the year. At each stop, he played the "best ball" of the two best players in the town, or a top professional in a singles contest. He lost only 13 out of 65 best-ball matches and dropped only one singles match. In grand fashion, Vardon won the 1900 U.S. Open (even though he whiffed at a one-inch putt on the final hole). Vardon prevailed by two strokes and outdistanced the nearest American professional, David Ball, by 10 shots.

The 1900 tour has rightfully been credited with creating the first significant interest in golf in the United States. Vardon would return again to the United States, in 1913, for another exhibition tour. With this trip, he was again a factor in arousing interest in golf by Americans, but this time because he lost a competition. That year, Vardon (and his compatriot, Ted Ray) were defeated in a playoff for the U.S. Open by a young, unknown American amateur named Francis Ouimet. Had Ouimet beaten someone of less repute than Vardon (and Ray), his victory would hardly have gotten the acclaim it did—acclaim that spurred one of the biggest booms in American golf annals.

Vardon, along with his brothers, got into golf as a caddie. He played his first golf at the age of eight when he, his brothers, and other young boys built a course of their own. (Most of the holes were in the 50-yard-long range.) He made his own clubs—the heads of oak, the faces covered with strips of tin, the shafts of blackthorn branches. The "balls" were marbles.

Vardon followed his father into gardening work. But his first job was for a retired Army officer who was a golf fanatic, and he gave Vardon his first set of real golf clubs. Not long after, in his early 20s, Vardon followed his brother into professional golf. In 1896, the 26-year-old Vardon won his first British Open title, defeating defending champion J. H. Taylor by four strokes in a 36-hole playoff.

Vardon remained at the top of the game for the next 25 years. Much of his competitive record has been lost, but it is known that at one point he had won 14 straight tournaments in Great Britain.

Putting wasn't Vardon's strong suit. "I think I know as well as anybody how not to do it," he once said. However, Vardon's accuracy is the stuff of legend. It was said that if he played the same course in the afternoon that he played that morning, the second time around he hit out of his morning divots. Perhaps not, but such stories usually have some basis in fact. Whatever the case, Vardon was an exceptionally straight shooter—in manner as well as with his golf clubs. He was a taciturn man, soft-spoken but trenchant when the moment arose. A young Bobby Jones was paired with Vardon in a qualifying round for the 1920 U.S. Open. And after Jones topped a simple pitch shot, he asked Vardon, "Did you ever see a worse shot in your life?" To which Vardon answered, simply and honestly, "No."

CAREER HIGHLIGHTS

Achievements: Won 1896, 1898, 1899, 1903, 1911, and 1914 British Opens; 1900 U.S. Open. Only player to have won six British Open titles. Namesake of Vardon Trophy, awarded annually to the Tour player with the lowest stroke average; and Vardon Grip, still used by most modern golfers. Once won 14 consecutive tournaments in his native Great Britain. Member of PGA/World Golf Hall of Fame.

KEN VENTURI

○ ○ ○

His shining moment came in a courageous victory while battling heat exhaustion at the 1964 U.S. Open, but it should also be noted that Ken Venturi was one of the Tour's best players during the late 1950s. He won 14 tournaments in a PGA Tour career that ended prematurely due to a circulatory problem in his hands.

Venturi, born in San Francisco in 1931, was runner-up in the first U.S. Junior championship in 1948. Venturi nearly won the 1956 Masters as an amateur, taking a four-stroke lead into the final round before collapsing with an 80 in windy conditions to finish second, one stroke behind Jack Burke Jr.

Venturi, who turned pro later in 1956, would come close in two more Masters. He finished fourth, two strokes off the lead, in 1958, and he was second by one stroke in 1960 thanks to Arnold Palmer's finish of birdies on the last two holes. Nonetheless, Venturi finished in the top 10 on the money list in his first four years on Tour, 1957 through 1960, winning 10 events in that span.

Venturi had gained a reputation as one of the best iron players in the game. However, after 1960, he decided to make some changes to gain more length off the tee. His game lost consistency and he went into a deep slump. Venturi began to return to form in 1964, but he was still a long shot at the U.S. Open. Venturi was two strokes behind after a third-round 66 at Congressional. By the end of the round, the 100-degree heat was beginning to get to him, and there was some question whether Venturi would be able to complete the 36-hole final day. With a doctor following him, Venturi managed to get around with a closing 70 to win by four in one of the most inspiring performances in championship golf annals.

He won three more events in 1964, but the next year Venturi was struck by the circulatory problem. He had surgery and missed most of the campaign. He came back with one win in 1966 and played well at times during the 1967 season, but the ailment still dogged him. Venturi, who finished as high as second in Tour earnings twice during his career, soon retired from competition and became a fixture in the CBS broadcast booth.

Career Highlights

Earnings: $268,293
PGA Tour Victories: 14
Achievements: Won 1964 U.S. Open in dramatic fashion, shooting 66–70 on the 36-hole final day while battling heat exhaustion. Finished second in 1956 and 1960 Masters, the former as an amateur. Second in Tour earnings in 1960 and third in 1958. Veteran CBS golf broadcaster.

LANNY WADKINS

○ ○ ○

KNOWN FOR HIS ATTACKING STYLE and competitive nature, Lanny Wadkins has carved out a career that included 21 PGA Tour victories through 1997. His aggressive play might have hurt him in the majors—he won only one, the 1977 PGA Championship—but Wadkins won more tournaments than any player of his generation except Tom Watson and Johnny Miller and was also an acclaimed international player.

Wadkins was already hailed as a coming star when he joined the Tour in 1972 at age 22. The Virginia native had won the 1970 U.S. Amateur, played on the Walker Cup teams of 1969 and 1971, and finished second in a Tour event, the 1970 Heritage Classic, as an amateur. He lived up to his promise in his first two years on Tour, finishing 10th and fifth on the money list while winning three times.

Wadkins then began a roller-coaster period of eight years in which he was either near the top of the money list or out of the top 50. He was in a three-year slump before winning the 1977 PGA, where he took advantage of Gene Littler's back-nine collapse at Pebble Beach to win on the third hole of sudden-death. Wadkins later won the World Series of Golf to finish third on the money list. He won twice more in 1979, including an impressive showing in nasty winds at the Tournament Players Championship.

After two more off years in 1980 and '81, Wadkins became a more consistent player and posted 14 wins from 1982 through '92. He won three events each in 1982 and '85, and two in 1983 and '88. He was the PGA Player of the Year in 1985. Wadkins was a runner-up in the PGA Championship in 1982, '84, and '87, losing a playoff to Larry Nelson in the latter year. He finished third in the Masters in 1990, '91, and '93.

Wadkins gained his reputation as a competitor thanks largely to his record in the Ryder Cup Matches. Playing on eight U.S. Ryder Cup teams, he went 20–11–3. Only Arnold Palmer has won more Ryder Cup Matches (22). Wadkins also served as captain of the U.S. team in the 1995 Ryder Cup Matches.

CAREER HIGHLIGHTS
Earnings: $6,093,850
PGA Tour Victories: 21
Achievements: Won 1977 PGA Championship; 1979 Players Championship; 1970 U.S. Amateur Championship. Tour Player of the Year in 1985. Won three events in 1982 and 1985. Captained 1995 U.S. Ryder Cup team after having played on the squad eight times.

Art Wall

○ ○ ○

For one year—1959—Art Wall stood atop the golf world. At the age of 35, the unassuming Pennsylvania native won four tournaments, including the Masters, finished second in six more, and led the PGA Tour money list with $53,167. He stepped aside from the summit to let Arnold Palmer take over the next year, but continued with a long and productive career that produced 14 victories and 29 runner-up finishes. One of the few pros to win past age 50, he won his last Tour event at age 51.

Wall didn't turn pro until he was 25 years old and joined the Tour a year later, in 1950. His first victory came in the 1953 Fort Wayne Open, beginning a streak of 12 straight years where he finished first or second in at least one tournament. His second victory came in the 1954 Tournament of Champions, but it was in 1957 that he hit his prime.

Wall finished seventh on the money list in 1957 and fifth in 1958 before rising to the No. 1 spot in 1959. Never a long hitter, Wall was among the game's most consistent players. He was also noted for his accurate putting stroke. Between 1957 and 1959, he posted a total of 52 top-10 finishes. He won the Bing Crosby Pro-Am and Azalea

Open early in 1959 to head into the Masters on a good note. There, he trailed co-leaders Palmer and Stan Leonard by six strokes heading into the final round before accomplishing one of the most spectacular finishes in Masters history. Wall birdied five of the last six holes to close with a 66 and win by one over Cary Middlecoff. Wall won the Vardon Trophy and PGA Player of the Year honors that season.

The victories dried up in the 1960s, but Wall continued to carve out a good living, capped by his victory in the 1975 Greater Milwaukee Open at the age of 51. He became one of the oldest players ever to win a Tour event. A few years later he participated in (and lost) a memorable playoff with partner Tommy Bolt to Roberto de Vicenzo and Julius Boros in the 1979 Liberty Mutual Legends of Golf, an event that is credited with helping to launch the Senior Tour. Wall and Bolt won the Legends in 1980.

Career Highlights

Earnings: $638,816
PGA Tour Victories: 14
Achievements: Won 1959 Masters; 1960 Canadian Open; 1954 Tournament of Champions. Vardon Trophy winner and Player of the Year in 1959, when he led Tour in earnings. Member of U.S. Ryder Cup team from 1957 to 1961. Won 1975 Greater Milwaukee Open at age 51.

TOM WATSON

○ ○ ○

ONLY ONE GOLFER EVER CAME close to challenging Jack Nicklaus as the most dominant player in golf. That was Tom Watson, who from 1974 to '83 won eight major championships and 28 tournaments overall on the PGA Tour. In the same time frame, Nicklaus won six majors (and 18 PGA Tour events). To be sure, Nicklaus had been on the tournament circuit for 12 years when Watson won for the first time on the PGA Tour—the 1974 Western Open—and had cut back on his schedule of appearances to some extent, but Nicklaus's capacity for great golf, and the longevity of it, was so colossal that the comparison between the two is valid.

Thomas Sturges Watson was born in Kansas City, Missouri, in 1949. Although a most promising golfer from the start, Watson did not have an especially remarkable amateur career. He won his share of smaller amateur events, but none of the prestigious ones. And in playing for the Stanford University team, he did not shine as his future record would suggest he should have.

It took him three years on the PGA Tour, which he joined in 1971, to win for the first time. When he did have a chance to win a major title, he showed a tendency to weaken down the stretch.

He led the 1974 U.S. Open by a shot after three rounds, but he finished with a 79 to end up tied for fifth. The next year, in the Open, he opened with rounds of 67–68 to take a three-stroke lead, but he shot 78–77 to finish in a tie for ninth. After this, he was considered something of a choker. He proceeded to put the slur to rest, with a fury.

In 1975, Watson broke through to win the British Open, in a playoff with Jack Newton. Winning his first major in Great Britain was fitting, for Watson always had a particular affinity for playing there. The often wet weather smacked of the golf he played growing up in Missouri. Also, he had always expressed a fondness for the grand traditions of the old Scots' game. Indeed, he would win the British Open five times (1975, '77, '80, '82, and '83). Only one other player, Peter Thomson, has won that honored title that many times in the modern era.

All golfers' careers in the Nicklaus Era were naturally measured against Jack's, and Watson had two significant high points. In 1982 at Pebble Beach, it appeared Nicklaus would win his fifth U.S. Open. But Watson chipped in from a heavy lie on the fringe at the 17th green for a birdie-2 and a one-shot lead, which he maintained. The chip-in was an unforgettable moment. But the two of them had already gone one better.

In the 1977 British Open at Turnberry, Scotland, Watson's victory over Nicklaus was the most dynamic one-on-one confrontation in golf history. They both shot 68–70 in rounds one and two, then the fireworks began. Watson and Nicklaus, playing together, matched 65s in round three. Again together for the final 18, they had left the field so far behind that when they came to the 72nd hole, either one of them could 10-putt and finish runner-up.

> *"The person I fear most in the last two rounds is myself."*
> —Tom Watson

Leading by a stroke going to the last hole, Watson drove perfectly in the fairway. Nicklaus drove into deep gorse. Watson played an 8-iron approach to within 30 inches of the hole. Miraculously, Nicklaus freed his ball from the thicket with an 8-iron, the ball finishing 32 feet from the cup. He then ran the putt in for a round of 66. He had beaten the British Open 72-hole scoring record by seven shots—and still lost. Watson holed for a 65.

Watson also won two Masters, both in duels with Nicklaus. In the final round in 1977, Nicklaus caught up with Watson at the 13th hole. But when Watson holed a 20-foot birdie putt at 17, Nicklaus wilted (at 18), and Watson won by two. He won it again in 1981 by two over Nicklaus and Johnny Miller.

Watson would continue his powerful, well-thought-out golf through 1984, when he won three times on the PGA Tour, but then his game went into a steep decline. It was almost as if all the bold putting that was his trademark had caught up with his nerves. His putting approach continued to be aggressive, but all of a sudden he could no longer make the three- and four-footers coming back. Perhaps he needed Nicklaus to inspire him, but by the mid-1980s Jack was finally beginning to wind down his competitive career.

Interestingly, while Watson's ball-striking got better and better—his tendency toward wildness off the tee had been well tamed—his putting from short distances under ultimate pressure got worse and worse. He became a rather sympathetic figure as he missed one after another in the clutch, and a new generation of younger stars was beginning to emerge. He continued to fight the good fight, though, and in 1996 won for the first time in nine years. Ironically, the victory came at the Memorial Tournament, an event begun by, and played on a course designed by, Jack Nicklaus.

CAREER HIGHLIGHTS
Earnings: $7,833,351
PGA Tour Victories: 33
Achievements: Won 1975, 1977, 1980, 1982, and 1983 British Opens; 1977 and 1981 Masters; 1982 U.S. Open. Captured at least three events per year from 1977 through 1982. Vardon Trophy winner in 1977, 1978, and 1979. Led Tour in earnings four years in a row from 1977 to 1980 and in 1984. Six-time Player of the Year. Captained 1993 Ryder Cup team. Member of PGA/World Golf Hall of Fame.

Tom Weiskopf

○ ○ ○

He will forever be burdened with the label "unfulfilled potential," but Tom Weiskopf nonetheless had a very good career on the PGA Tour with 15 victories between 1968 and '82. Many felt that Weiskopf, blessed with enormous talent and a beautiful golf swing, could have achieved more. Two things held him back. He battled fits of temper that sometimes caused him to get in his own way on the golf course, and, perhaps more important, he never felt strongly driven to succeed.

Weiskopf joined the Tour in 1965 out of Ohio State University and broke through with his first two victories in 1968, when he finished third on the money list. He also ranked third in 1973 and '75. For a three-month stretch in 1973, Weiskopf was the best player in the game. In May, he won the Colonial Invitational and was second in Atlanta. In June, he won the Kemper Open, won in Philadelphia, and finished third in the U.S. Open, which was won by Johnny Miller. In July, Weiskopf captured what was to be his only major title, outdueling Miller in a two-man battle at the British Open, leading from start to finish.

Weiskopf came close in many other majors. He finished second four times in a span of seven years at the Masters, in 1969, '72, '74, and '75. The most painful was in 1975, when Weiskopf held the lead until Jack Nicklaus ran in a long birdie putt on the 16th and claimed a one-stroke victory. In addition to his third-place finish in the 1973 U.S. Open, he finished in the top four in that event four straight years—second in 1976, third in '77, fourth in '78, and fourth in '79. He also tied the U.S. Open 18-hole record with a 63 in 1980. Weiskopf was third in the 1975 PGA Championship and fourth in 1978.

Weiskopf's last multiple-win campaign came in 1975, when he had two victories. He quit the Tour in 1983 at age 41, partly because of a shoulder injury and partly to pursue a career in golf architecture. Weiskopf has enjoyed success on the Senior Tour since 1992, including a win in the 1995 U.S. Senior Open.

CAREER HIGHLIGHTS

Earnings: $2,241,688 (PGA); $1,683,215 (SR)
Tour Victories: 15 (PGA); 4 (SR)
Achievements: Won 1973 British Open; 1995 U.S. Senior Open; 1971, 1973, and 1977 Kemper Opens. Four-time Masters runner-up. Tied for second in 1976 U.S. Open. Captured four Tour events during eight-week span in 1973. Member of U.S. Ryder Cup teams in 1973 and 1975.

Joyce Wethered

○ ○ ○

WHILE IT IS IMPOSSIBLE to compare her accomplishments to those of the professionals of the latter half of the 20th century, one could make a case for Joyce Wethered as the greatest woman player of all time. Bobby Jones once called her the best golfer—male or female—he had ever seen. She won the English Amateur all five times she played in it and won the British Amateur four times in six tries, losing in the finals and semifinals on the other occasions.

Wethered, born in 1901, learned the game at age 17 from her brother, Roger, who was one of England's top amateurs. Accustomed to playing with strong male players, Wethered developed a swing that powered the ball past the other top women amateurs of the time.

Two years after she began to play the game, Wethered entered the 1920 English Amateur just for fun. She found herself in the final against Cecil Leitch, then Britain's best player. Wethered defeated her, 2 & 1, to win the event for the first of five straight years. Leitch gained some revenge by beating Wethered in the finals of the 1921 British and French Amateurs, but from then on Wethered ruled. In the British championship, Wethered won the 1922 final over Leitch, 9 & 7, lost in the semifinals in 1923, and won in 1924 and '25.

Wethered then retired from championship golf, much like Jones a few years later, with little left to accomplish and having grown tired of the competition. However, she returned to the British championship one more time—in 1929 at St. Andrews. The final was a classic between Wethered and America's best, Glenna Collett, with Wethered prevailing, 3 & 1. In 11 English and British Amateurs, Wethered played 71 matches and won 69.

Wethered didn't stop playing golf completely. She played in the 1932 Curtis Cup and continued to enter the Worplesdon Mixed Foursomes, winning it eight times from 1922 through 1936 with seven different partners. In 1935, she made her only appearances in the U.S., going on an exhibition tour with Gene Sarazen, Horton Smith, and Babe Didrikson. Wethered is said to have outscored Didrickson on that tour while breaking several course records.

Career Highlights
Achievements: Won 1920, 1921, 1922, 1923, and 1924 English Amateur Championships; 1922, 1924, 1925, and 1929 British Amateur Championships. Competed in 1932 Curtis Cup. Winner of eight Worplesdon Mixed Foursomes titles with seven different partners. Member of PGA/World Golf Hall of Fame.

KATHY WHITWORTH

○ ○ ○

IN A WORLD WITH A COLLECTIVE attention span that's roughly the length of a television commercial, Kathy Whitworth's career may not seem noteworthy. But for those who understand and appreciate the strength and dedication involved in upholding a well-honed athletic talent—and the determination to maintain a high standard for achievement for over four decades—Whitworth will always be impressive.

Kathrynne Ann Whitworth was born in Monahans, Texas, in 1939 and raised in Jal, New Mexico, where her father and mother ran a hardware store. A natural athlete, and inclined to play sports despite the social stigma this meant for someone of her gender in her generation, she took up golf at the age of 15 and showed enough promise from the start that a teacher of the highest repute took her on as a student—the great Harvey Penick. At 19, Whitworth won her second consecutive New Mexico State Amateur championship and left a college in Odessa, Texas, where she had a golf scholarship, to turn pro.

Whitworth's father and two businessmen friends promised her a three-year sponsorship on the LPGA Tour, which was just beginning to get on its feet. Moreover, Wilson Sporting Goods signed her to a contract that included paying her expenses plus a stipend for doing golf clinics, and she was on her way. Whitworth seemed set to light up the women's golf world right from the start, but her fuse happened to be a slow one. In her first season on the circuit, 1959, she entered 26 events and won a grand total of $1,217 on the basis of a scoring average of 80.30. Nevertheless, she hung in there to become the biggest winner in American golf history.

Tutored by teaching pros Harvey Penick and Hardy Loudermilk, Whitworth crafted a steady, consistent swing and tremendous accuracy.

It is difficult to imagine that the tall, slender, tautly muscled woman fans saw for so many years weighed over 200 pounds when she was in high school. "I'd probably be the fat lady in the circus if it hadn't been for golf," Whitworth once said. "It kept me out of the refrigerator." As she gradually pared down to her playing weight, 145, which she maintained throughout her career, her game improved accordingly. In 1962, Whitworth won her first LPGA tournament, the Kelly Girl Open, and won one more that season. She was a workhorse, playing an average of 25 tournaments a year from 1959 through 1991.

Although not a very long hitter of the ball, Whitworth was long enough for her time. More important, she put together a very functional and repeatable golf swing. It wasn't the kind that lasts for the ages, and it wasn't the flowing poetry in motion of Mickey Wright, but neither was it Nancy Lopez's exotic manifestation. It was right down the middle, which is where Whitworth played most of her golf. The Whitworth swing held up very well.

In 1963, Whitworth won eight tournaments. She had a quiet '64, with only one victory, but in 1965 she won eight more times, including her first major, the Titleholders Championship, which she won again the next year. In 1967, she won eight events including two more majors—the LPGA Championship and the Western Open. She was on a long and good roll, but after her 1973 season, when she won seven times, the physical and emotional strain of playing at such a high level for a decade did take its toll. She even had a notion to pack it in. But it was only a notion, it was not Whitworth, and she came back to win again and again. In all, she won 88 LPGA events, which is the all-time record among both men and women.

It is a curious coincidence that just as Sam Snead on the men's side won more tournaments than any other of his gender (81 officials plus a British Open) but never won the U.S. Open, so it was with Kathy Whitworth, who never could take the U.S. Women's Open. And just as in Snead's case, the missing major in her record doesn't at all diminish Whitworth's career.

What's more, it should be added that while accumulating her competitive record, Whitworth held at one time or another every LPGA administrative office at least once—from treasurer to three-time president—a time- and energy-consuming labor that Snead and the other greats never had to take on. Whitworth joined the LPGA circuit in the days when it was run by the players themselves, with everyone pitching in to lure sponsors, organize the events, and in some cases even cut the holes. And yet, while performing her various organizational duties, she was the leading money winner eight times and won the Vare Trophy seven times. Though her winning purses were as low as $800, Whitworth won so often that she became the first woman to reach $1 million in career prize money.

CAREER HIGHLIGHTS
Earnings: $1,731,770
LPGA Tour Victories: 88
Achievements: Won 1965 and 1966 Titleholders Championships; 1967, 1971, and 1975 LPGA Championships; 1967 Western Open. Holds record for men's and women's U.S. Tours with 88 wins. Became first LPGA Player to earn $1 million. Led Tour in earnings eight times. Won seven Vare Trophies and seven LPGA Player of the Year awards. Member of LPGA Hall of Fame and PGA/World Golf Hall of Fame.

CRAIG WOOD

○ ○ ○

Until he won the Masters and U.S. Open in 1941 at the age of 39, Craig Wood was the hard-luck golfer of his era. Before then, he had finished second five times in major championships. Worse, four of those losses had come in playoffs, and he was victimized by some extraordinary feats by his competitors.

Wood, born in upstate New York, scored his first Tour victory in 1928. He had his first runner-up finish in a major five years later, when he lost the British Open in a playoff against Denny Shute. Wood finished second in the first two Masters, in 1934 and '35. After finishing one stroke behind Horton Smith in the inaugural event, Wood was in the clubhouse with a three-stroke lead the next year only to have Gene Sarazen tie him by holing a 4-wood for a double eagle on the 15th hole. Sarazen won the 36-hole playoff, 144–149. Wood was runner-up to Paul Runyan in the final of the 1934 PGA Championship in a scheduled 36-hole match that went two extra holes in Wood's home state.

It looked like Wood might get a break in the 1939 U.S. Open when Sam Snead blew the title on the 72nd hole, leaving Wood, Shute, and Byron Nelson tied for first. Wood shot a 68 in the 18-hole playoff, but so did Nelson, requiring another 18-hole playoff between the two of them. Nelson holed a 1-iron shot on the fourth hole and went on to win, 70–73.

Finally, in 1941, things went Wood's way. He grabbed a five-stroke lead in the first round of the Masters with a 66 and held on to beat Nelson by three. Wood considered withdrawing in the first round of that year's U.S. Open due to a back injury, but he hung in and ended up winning by three strokes over Shute.

Wood finished his competitive career with 21 victories, the last of which came in 1944. He was a very long hitter, evidenced by a wind-aided drive of 430 yards during the 1933 British Open at St. Andrews.

A Ryder Cup regular from 1931 to 1935, Wood also enjoyed a successful career as a club professional. He held that post at famed Winged Foot Golf Club for several years before moving to the Bahamas.

Career Highlights
PGA Tour Victories: 21
Achievements: Won 1941 Masters; 1941 U.S. Open. Finished among top three in all four major championships. Drove a bunker 430 yards out during 1933 British Open at St. Andrews. Member of U.S. Ryder Cup teams in 1931, 1933, and 1935. Long-time professional at Winged Foot Golf Club.

TIGER WOODS

○ ○ ○

Not since Jack Nicklaus came onto the scene three-and-a-half decades earlier had the golf world seen anything like Tiger Woods. Like Nicklaus, Woods compiled an outstanding amateur record, and instant success was expected of him when he hit the PGA Tour. Also like Jack, Tiger delivered, winning a major championship in his first year as a professional. And, like the young Nicklaus, Woods hit the ball so much farther than other pros that he seemed to be playing a different game.

In fact, while it can't be known whether he will have the staying power to challenge Nicklaus's record total of 18 major professional championships, Woods made an even bigger impact on the game in his first year as a pro than the Golden Bear did. For one thing, Woods is part African American (also part Asian and a small part American Indian), which is significant because there were no black players on the Tour full-time when he arrived. Also, he plays an exciting, attacking style and has a charismatic smile. When Woods is in a tournament, attendance and television ratings go through the roof. Woods has the kind of mass appeal that brings new players to the game, much like Arnold Palmer had.

If any golfer were ever destined for greatness from an early age, it was Woods. Tiger, who grew up in the Los Angeles suburbs and learned to swing the club by mimicking his father, Earl, made his first trip to the driving range at just 18 months. At age two, he won a 10-and-under tournament and appeared on the *Mike Douglas Show*. At eight, he broke 80 for the first time. At 12, he broke 70. At 14, he started winning national junior tournaments for players 17 and under.

Woods's greatest amateur accomplishments came in USGA events. Before him, no player had won the U.S. Junior Amateur more than once. Woods won it three times in a row, beginning at age 15 (the youngest ever to win the title). He followed up on that by becoming the youngest-ever U.S. Amateur champion, at 18. When he won the U.S. Amateur again at 19 and 20, he became the first player ever to win that event three straight times.

Many of those wins came in dramatic fashion. In his third U.S. Junior victory, Woods was two down with two holes to play. He birdied them both, and then won on the first extra hole of sudden death. He captured his first U.S. Amateur by coming back from six down after 13 holes of the 36-hole final to take a 2-up victory over Trip Kuehne. He captured his third by charging from five down after 18 to win on the 38th hole against Steve Scott.

By then, Woods had completed two years at Stanford University, winning one NCAA Championship, and speculation in the golf world centered on how soon he would turn pro. Woods took that step immediately following his third U.S. Amateur victory, encouraged by many top pros telling him he was ready for the Tour and sensing that college and amateur golf would no longer hold enough interest for him. Nike immediately gave him a $40 million endorsement contract. At the time, many wondered if Woods deserved it, since he hadn't yet proved himself on the Tour. He quickly demonstrated that he was worth every penny—and more.

"I think he can win almost anywhere. I don't think there's anything that can stop him."
—ARNOLD PALMER, ON TIGER WOODS

Playing in only eight tournaments in 1996 after turning pro at the end of August, he won twice (the Las Vegas Invitational and Walt Disney World/Oldsmobile Classic), finished third twice, and collected $790,594. He was a phenomenon in every sense of the word. Even his fellow pros were in awe of his distance off the tee, accomplished with the efficiency of his swing rather than brute strength (he's 6'2", 155 pounds). And he brought the spectators flooding through the gates, particularly youngsters who wouldn't have otherwise been interested in golf.

Tigermania continued in 1997. He won the first tournament of the year, the Mercedes Championships, by nearly holing his tee shot to win a sudden-death playoff. At the Masters, he topped even the loftiest expectations by blowing away the field with a record 72-hole total of 270 to win by a record 12 strokes. By then, it was clear that the sky was the limit.

Woods went on to post two more 1997 victories, adding the Byron Nelson Classic and the Western Open to his résumé. He set a new Tour earnings standard by the midpoint of the season and finished the year as the first player to break the $2 million barrier in a single season. He ran away with 1997 Player of the Year honors and was a Ryder Cup headliner. Perhaps as remarkable as his wins is the fact Woods made the cut in his first 25 professional tournaments, a streak that ended at the Canadian Open.

CAREER HIGHLIGHTS

Earnings: $2,066,833
PGA Tour Victories: 4
Achievements: Won 1997 Masters; 1994, 1995, and 1996 U.S. Amateurs; 1991, 1992, and 1993 U.S. Junior Amateurs. First player to win three straight U.S. Amateurs and, at 18 in 1994, youngest ever to win the event. Set Masters scoring record and won by a record 12 strokes in 1997. *Sports Illustrated* Sportsman of the Year in 1996. Shot 48 for nine holes at age 3. Captured NCAA title in 1996.

MICKEY WRIGHT

○ ○ ○

IT IS USUALLY THE CASE THAT the greatest golfers do not swing by the "book," but succeed through guile and determination. On the other hand, most of those who do make a smooth and elegant classic swing, with everything falling into the right places, never possess the intangibles to reach the greatest heights. It follows then that if someone combines a perfect golf swing with an intense will to win, that someone is going to be very special. Such a person was Mary Kathryn "Mickey" Wright, who to this day is heralded as the all-time greatest woman golfer. Her record is proof of that. And thanks to film and video, golfers not born when Wright was in her prime are able to view and confirm for themselves her exquisite expression of the golfing art.

Wright was born in San Diego in 1935. At age nine, she played her first golf and "took to it like a duck," as Wright once recalled. Two years later, after she broke 100 for the first time, her picture appeared in a San Diego newspaper with a caption: "The Next Babe?" "From that time on, I was determined to become a professional golfer," said Wright. Her first formal instruction was with Johnny Bellante, who also got Gene Littler started.

When Wright was 14, she broke 70 for the first time and also won the Southern California Girls' Junior championship. The pro at that event was Harry Pressler, a highly regarded teacher, and Wright began taking lessons from him. It was he who was mainly responsible for shaping her swing. But Wright, an inveterate student of the golf swing, also worked with Stan Kertes (who taught Babe Zaharias to play) and Texas pro Earl Stewart. So she found the best teachers, to which she added her own intelligence and natural physical gifts. A tallish woman, she had a long swing arc and the powerful hand action at impact associated with men players. Both were sources of her considerable length off the tee. And, with her uncomplicated swing pattern, she was also very accurate—not to mention consistent.

As an amateur on the national level, Wright won the 1952 U.S. Girls' Junior and the '54 World Amateur. She was also the low amateur in the '54 U.S. Women's Open. She attended Stanford for a year, at the insistence of her dad, but was not happy. She just wanted to play pro golf. Her father could not ignore her accomplishments and relented. He gave Mickey $1,000 to get started, and the great odyssey began. She turned pro in 1955 and won her first LPGA tournament in '56. She won thrice in '57, but in the U.S. Open made, in retrospect, a poor showing with rounds of 89–82–81–80. The next year, she made up for it in a major way.

> *Wright began practicing on a driving range at age nine and played her first round two years later.*

In 1958, Wright won three regular Tour events plus the LPGA Championship and the U.S. Women's Open. In the latter, she became at 23 the youngest winner of the championship. She led after every round, finished five shots ahead of Louise Suggs, and set a new Open scoring record with a 2-under-par 290—one better than Babe Zaharias scored in 1954. The next year, Wright defended her U.S. Open title and broke her own scoring record by three shots. She would win the Open four times and claim a total of 13 majors.

Wright's competitive record is filled with striking achievements: second in all-time LPGA victories with 82; winner of three majors in one season—the 1961 U.S. Women's Open, LPGA, and Titleholders; twice recorded four consecutive victories on the LPGA Tour (1962 and '63); and won 13 times in 1963, a stratospheric record in the Byron Nelson class that many feel will never be equaled.

Wright did all her marvelous playing from 1956 to '69, then stopped playing regularly owing to some real and, some would say, self-designed reasons: She had developed a growth on her left foot, and after an operation played all her golf in tennis shoes. She also suffered from sheer exhaustion; sponsors threatened to cancel tournaments if she didn't appear, and in acceding for the good of the circuit she played more than anyone should. She also claimed an adverse reaction to the sun, as well as an aversion to flying (which became necessary as the LPGA Tour grew, thanks in good part to her). Finally, Wright had an abiding modesty that never allowed her enjoy her celebrity. A quiet, introspective woman with a range of interests outside of golf (literature, music, fishing, the stock market), she became something of a recluse.

In 1979, however, Wright competed in the Coca-Cola Classic and got into a five-way playoff that was eventually won by 22-year-old Nancy Lopez. Wright, at 44, hadn't competed consistently for a decade, but she outhit Lopez off the tee and outplayed the three others in the overtime play before losing on the second extra hole to a birdie—if "losing" is the right word for it.

CAREER HIGHLIGHTS
Earnings: $368,770
LPGA Tour Victories: 82
Achievements: Won 1958, 1959, 1961, and 1964 U.S. Women's Opens; 1958, 1960, 1961, and 1963 LPGA Championships; 1961 and 1962 Titleholders Championships; 1962, 1963, and 1966 Western Opens. Won four consecutive LPGA events in both 1962 and 1963. Posted 13 Tour wins in 1963. Vare Trophy winner each year from 1960 to 1964. Member of LPGA Hall of Fame and PGA/World Golf Hall of Fame.

BABE DIDRIKSON ZAHARIAS

○ ○ ○

IT IS THE RARE ATHLETE WHO CAN master more than one sport, and even more so when the transition is to golf. Mildred "Babe" Didrikson Zaharias managed it, although in considering her immense athletic talent, it is not that surprising.

Didrikson was an All-America basketball player in high school, a proficient swimmer and diver, an expert rifle shot, a boxer, a speed-ball softball pitcher, a top-notch bowler, and a tennis player of championship caliber. Track and field, however, was where she made her initial impact on the sports world. In the 1932 national track and field championships, she placed first in eight of 10 events. But two weeks later the young Texan became an international star. In the Olympics in Los Angeles, Didrikson placed first in two events and a controversial second in another. She set a new world record in the javelin throw, broke the old world record for the 80-meter hurdles in winning her heat, then broke that record in the finals. She tied for first in the high jump but settled for silver after being penalized.

Cashing in on her newfound fame, Didrikson played the vaudeville circuit for a time, dancing and playing the harmonica. (At age seven, she had been a harmonica soloist on a Texas radio station, and she was a professional-level tap dancer.) More interested in sports, Babe left show business and played on a professional basketball team as well as some exhibition baseball. She pitched for the House of David team and threw an inning's worth for the Philadelphia Phillies in an exhibition game against the Brooklyn Dodgers.

> *"When I want to really blast one, I just loosen my girdle and let 'er fly," Babe said.*

Then, in 1934, Didrikson turned to golf, which she had been playing on and off for a number of years. In 1935, Didrikson (she would add Zaharias to her name in 1938 after marrying George Zaharias, a professional wrestler) went on a golf exhibition swing with Gene Sarazen. Although not yet a finished golfer, she could hit the ball distances equal to that of many men players. Her power was a great attraction and amplified her nickname, "Babe," which came after she hit five home runs in a baseball game. "When I want to really blast one," she once said, "I just loosen my girdle and let 'er fly." However, if she was going to compete in golf at a championship level, she would have to refine the rest of her game. Zaharias took lessons from Stan Kertes, a fine, albeit unheralded, golf teacher in Chicago and Los Angeles. She practiced long and hard for a couple of years and began entering a few tournaments.

Born in Port Arthur, Texas, in 1911, the daughter of Norwegian immigrants, she was known as Babe Zaharias for most of her competitive golf career, which began in earnest during the World War II years. Declared a professional (for her baseball and basketball earnings) after winning the Women's Texas Invitational in 1935, her amateur status was reinstated in 1943, at her request. In 1945, she won her third Western Open. In 1946 and '47, she won 14 amateur tournaments in a row, including the '46 U.S. Women's Amateur and the '47 British Women's Amateur. She was the first American ever to claim victory in the latter, and afterward she again became a professional, this time for good.

In the late 1940s, Zaharias, Patty Berg, and Betty Hicks re-formed the Women's Professional Golf Association into the Ladies PGA, and they began developing its Tour. Zaharias was a major attraction by virtue of her excellent golf, but also as an outgoing, irrepressible personality. Her show-business instincts and background were never far from the surface. From 1948 through '55, Zaharias won 31 professional tournaments, including three U.S. Women's Opens.

Zaharias's professional golf career was actually rather short—only nine years—because her fabled physical capacities began to deteriorate. In 1952, she had surgery for a strangulated hernia. Then, in 1953, she was operated on for cancer. Her doctor said she would never play championship golf again. Of course, he underestimated the Babe. Three months later she was back on Tour, and the following year she won five times, including her third U.S. Open. In '54, she won the Vare Trophy and was second on the money list. She was named the A.P. Woman Athlete of the First Half of the 20th Century, and she was probably the best woman athlete of all time.

The only thing Zaharias couldn't beat was cancer. After the first surgery for the malady, she played winning golf into 1955, when she won twice on the Tour. But in June of that year, she was again operated on, and this time she was unable to come back. She died in September 1956, at the age of 42.

CAREER HIGHLIGHTS

Earnings: $66,237
LPGA Tour Victories: 31
Achievements: Won 1948, 1950, and 1954 U.S. Women's Opens; 1947, 1950, and 1952 Titleholders Championships; 1940, 1944, 1945, and 1950 Western Opens. Founder of LPGA. Vare Trophy winner in 1954. Led Tour in earnings four straight years from 1948 to 1951. Captured 1954 U.S. Women's Open just months after her first cancer operation. Member of LPGA Hall of Fame and PGA/World Golf Hall of Fame.

HISTORICAL RECORDS

○ ○ ○

PGA Tour
Grand Slam Summary

Year	Masters	US Open	Brit. Open	PGA
1934	H. Smith	Dutra	Cotton	Runyan
1935	Sarazen	Parks	Perry	Revolta
1936	H. Smith	Manero	Padgham	Shute
1937	B. Nelson	Guldahl	Cotton	Shute
1938	Picard	Guldahl	Whitcombe	Runyan
1939	Guldahl	B. Nelson	Burton	Picard
1940	Demaret	Little	—	B. Nelson
1941	Wood	Wood	—	Ghezzi
1942	B. Nelson	—	—	Snead
1943	—	—	—	—
1944	—	—	—	Hamilton
1945	—	—	—	B. Nelson
1946	Keiser	Mangrum	Snead	Hogan
1947	Demaret	Worsham	F. Daly	Ferrier
1948	Harmon	Hogan	Cotton	Hogan
1949	Snead	Middlecoff	Locke	Snead
1950	Demaret	Hogan	Cotton	Harper
1951	Hogan	Hogan	Faulkner	Snead
1952	Snead	Boros	Locke	Turnesa
1953	Hogan	Hogan	Hogan	Burkemo
1954	Snead	Furgol	Thomson	Harbert
1955	Middlecoff	Fleck	Thomson	Ford
1956	Burke	Middlecoff	Thomson	Burke
1957	Ford	Mayer	Locke	L. Herbert
1958	Palmer	Bolt	Thomson	Finsterwald
1959	Wall	Casper	Player	Rosburg
1960	Palmer	Palmer	Nagle	J. Herbert
1961	Player	Littler	Palmer	J. Barber
1962	Palmer	Nicklaus	Palmer	Player
1963	Nicklaus	Boros	Charles	Nicklaus
1964	Palmer	Venturi	Lema	Nichols
1965	Nicklaus	Player	Thomson	Marr
1966	Nicklaus	Casper	Nicklaus	Geiberger

Year				
1967	Brewer	Nicklaus	De Vicenzo	January
1968	Goalby	Trevino	Player	Boros
1969	Archer	Moody	Jacklin	Floyd
1970	Casper	Jacklin	Nicklaus	Stockton
1971	Coody	Trevino	Trevino	Nicklaus
1972	Nicklaus	Nicklaus	Trevino	Player
1973	Aaron	J. Miller	Weiskopf	Nicklaus
1974	Player	Irwin	Player	Trevino
1975	Nicklaus	L. Graham	T. Watson	Nicklaus
1976	Floyd	J. Pate	Miller	Stockton
1977	T. Watson	H. Green	T. Watson	L. Wadkins
1978	Player	North	Nicklaus	Mahaffey
1979	Zoeller	Irwin	Ballesteros	D. Graham
1980	Ballesteros	Nicklaus	T. Watson	Nicklaus
1981	T. Watson	D. Graham	Rogers	L. Nelson
1982	Stadler	T. Watson	T. Watson	Floyd
1983	Ballesteros	L. Nelson	T. Watson	Sutton
1984	Crenshaw	Zoeller	Ballesteros	Trevino
1985	Langer	North	Lyle	H. Green
1986	Nicklaus	Floyd	Norman	Tway
1987	Mize	S. Simpson	Faldo	L. Nelson
1988	Lyle	Strange	Ballesteros	Sluman
1989	Faldo	Strange	Calcavecchia	Stewart
1990	Faldo	Irwin	Faldo	Grady
1991	Woosnam	Stewart	Baker-Finch	J. Daly
1992	Couples	Kite	Faldo	Price
1993	Langer	Janzen	Norman	Azinger
1994	Olazabal	Els	Price	Price
1995	Crenshaw	Pavin	Daly	Elkington
1996	Faldo	S. Jones	Lehman	Brooks
1997	Woods	Els	Leonard	Love

Career Tournament Wins

1) Sam Snead 81
2) Jack Nicklaus 70
3) Ben Hogan 63
4) Arnold Palmer 60
5) Byron Nelson 52
6) Billy Casper 51
7) Walter Hagen 40
  Cary Middlecoff 40
9) Gene Sarazen 38
10) Lloyd Mangrum 36
11) Tom Watson 33
12) Horton Smith 32
13) Harry Cooper 31
  Jimmy Demaret 31
15) Leo Diegel 30
16) Gene Littler 29
  Paul Runyan 29
18) Lee Trevino 27
19) Henry Picard 26
20) Tommy Armour 24
  Macdonald Smith 24
  Johnny Miller 24
23) Johnny Farrell 22
  Raymond Floyd 22
25) Gary Player 21
  Willie Macfarlane 21
  Bill Mehlhorn 21
  Lanny Wadkins 21

Career Tournament Wins *(continued)*

29) Craig Wood	21	Tom Kite	19
30) James Barnes	20	Ben Crenshaw	19
Doug Sanders	20	37) Julius Boros	18
Hale Irwin	20	Jim Ferrier	18
33) Doug Ford	19	Johnny Revolta	18
Hubert Green	19	Greg Norman	18

Career Money Leaders

1)	Greg Norman	$11,910,518
2)	Tom Kite	10,286,177
3)	Fred Couples	8,885,487
4)	Nick Price	8,794,431
5)	Mark O'Meara	8,506,774
6)	Davis Love III	8,470,982
7)	Payne Stewart	8,465,062
8)	Tom Watson	8,307,277
9)	Corey Pavin	8,130,356
10)	Scott Hoch	7,899,250
11)	Mark Calcavecchia	7,612,931
12)	Paul Azinger	7,451,410
13)	Curtis Strange	7,147,752
14)	Ben Crenshaw	7,064,604
15)	Craig Stadler	6,870,877
16)	Jay Haas	6,390,645
17)	Steve Elkington	6,328,138
18)	David Frost	6,299,819
19)	Lanny Wadkins	6,249,812
20)	John Cook	6,107,117
21)	Chip Beck	5,994,624
22)	Hale Irwin	5,902,306
23)	Bruce Lietzke	5,880,083
24)	Brad Faxon	5,842,619
25)	Tom Lehman	5,642,999
26)	Loren Roberts	5,642,104
27)	Jack Nicklaus	5,563,516
28)	Fuzzy Zoeller	5,401,176
29)	Lee Janzen	5,337,931
30)	Mark McCumber	5,290,798
31)	Raymond Floyd	5,269,595
32)	Gil Morgan	5,259,164
33)	Scott Simpson	5,210,150
34)	Larry Mize	5,149,716
35)	Jeff Sluman	5,145,364
36)	Hal Sutton	5,134,238
37)	Phil Mickelson	5,127,731
38)	Jim Gallagher Jr.	5,073,383

39) Peter Jacobsen	$4,969,692	
40) Mark Brooks	4,950,012	

Annual Money Leaders

1934	Paul Runyan	$6,767
1935	Johnny Revolta	9,543
1936	Horton Smith	7,682
1937	Harry Cooper	14,139
1938	Sam Snead	19,534
1939	Henry Picard	10,303
1940	Ben Hogan	10,655
1941	Ben Hogan	18,358
1942	Ben Hogan	13,143
1943	no statistics recorded	
1944	Byron Nelson	37,968
1945	Byron Nelson	63,336
1946	Ben Hogan	42,556
1947	Jimmy Demaret	27,937
1948	Ben Hogan	32,112
1949	Sam Snead	31,594
1950	Sam Snead	35,759
1951	Lloyd Mangrum	26,089
1952	Julius Boros	37,033
1953	Lew Worsham	34,002
1954	Bob Toski	65,820
1955	Julius Boros	63,122
1956	Ted Kroll	72,836
1957	Dick Mayer	65,835
1958	Arnold Palmer	42,608
1959	Art Wall	53,168
1960	Arnold Palmer	75,263
1961	Gary Player	64,540
1962	Arnold Palmer	81,448
1963	Arnold Palmer	128,230
1964	Jack Nicklaus	113,285
1965	Jack Nicklaus	140,752
1966	Billy Casper	121,945
1967	Jack Nicklaus	188,998
1968	Billy Casper	205,169
1969	Frank Beard	164,707
1970	Lee Trevino	157,038
1971	Jack Nicklaus	244,491
1972	Jack Nicklaus	320,542
1973	Jack Nicklaus	308,362
1974	Johnny Miller	353,022
1975	Jack Nicklaus	298,149
1976	Jack Nicklaus	266,439

Annual Money Leaders *(continued)*

Year	Player	Money
1977	Tom Watson	$310,653
1978	Tom Watson	362,429
1979	Tom Watson	462,636
1980	Tom Watson	530,808
1981	Tom Kite	375,699
1982	Craig Stadler	446,462
1983	Hal Sutton	426,668
1984	Tom Watson	476,260
1985	Curtis Strange	542,321
1986	Greg Norman	653,296
1987	Curtis Strange	925,941
1988	Curtis Strange	1,147,644
1989	Tom Kite	1,395,278
1990	Greg Norman	1,165,477
1991	Corey Pavin	979,430
1992	Fred Couples	1,344,188
1993	Nick Price	1,478,557
1994	Nick Price	1,499,927
1995	Greg Norman	1,654,959
1996	Tom Lehman	1,780,159
1997	Tiger Woods	2,066,833

Note: Total money listed from 1968 through 1974. Official money listed from 1975 through 1997. Byron Nelson's winnings in 1944 and 1945 were in war bonds.

LPGA TOUR

LPGA Grand Slam Summary

Year	LPGA	US Open	Titleholders	Western
1937	—	—	Berg	Hicks
1938	—	—	Berg	Barrett
1939	—	—	Berg	Dettweiler
1940	—	—	Hicks	Zaharias
1941	—	—	Kirby	Berg
1942	—	—	Kirby	Jameson
1943	—	—	—	Berg
1944	—	—	—	Zaharias
1945	—	—	—	Zaharias
1946	—	Berg	Suggs	Suggs
1947	—	Jameson	Zaharias	Suggs
1948	—	Zaharias	Berg	Berg
1949	—	Suggs	Kirk	Suggs
1950	—	Zaharias	Zaharias	Zaharias
1951	—	Rawls	O'Sullivan	Berg
1952	—	Suggs	Zaharias	Rawls
1953	—	Rawls	Berg	Suggs

Year	LPGA	US Open	du Maurier	D. Shore
1954	—	Zaharias	Suggs	Jameson
1955	Hanson	Crocker	Berg	Berg
1956	Hagge	Cornelius	Suggs	Hanson
1957	Suggs	Rawls	Berg	Berg
1958	Wright	Wright	Hanson	Berg
1959	Rawls	Wright	Suggs	Rawls
1960	Wright	Rawls	Crocker	Ziske
1961	Wright	Wright	Wright	Faulk
1962	Kimball	Lindstrom	Wright	Wright
1963	Wright	Mills	M. Smith	Wright
1964	Mills	Wright	M. Smith	Mann
1965	Haynie	Mann	Whitworth	Maxwell
1966	Ehret	Spuzich	Whitworth	Wright
1967	Whitworth	La-Coste	—	Whitworth
1968	Post	Berning	—	—
1969	Rawls	Caponi	—	—
1970	Englehorn	Caponi	—	—
1971	Whitworth	Carner	—	—
1972	Ahern	Berning	Palmer	—
1973	Mills	Berning	—	—
1974	Haynie	Haynie	—	—
1975	Whitworth	Palmer	—	—
1976	Burfeindt	Carner	—	—
1977	Higuchi	Stacy	—	—
Year	LPGA	US Open	du Maurier	D. Shore
1978	Lopez	Stacy	—	—
1979	Caponi	Britz	Alcott	—
1980	Little	Alcott	Bradley	—
1981	Caponi	Bradley	Stephenson	—
1982	Stephenson	Anderson	Haynie	—
1983	Sheehan	Stephenson	Stacy	Alcott
1984	Sheehan	Stacy	Inkster	Inkster
1985	Lopez	Baker	Bradley	Miller
1986	Bradley	Geddes	Bradley	Bradley
1987	Geddes	Davies	Rosenthal	King
1988	Turner	Neumann	Little	Alcott
1989	Lopez	King	Green	Inkster
1990	Daniel	King	Johnston	King
1991	Mallon	Mallon	Scranton	Alcott
1992	King	Sheehan	Steinhour	Mochrie
1993	Sheehan	Merten	Burton	Alfredsson
1994	Davies	Sheehan	Nause	Andrews
1995	Robbins	Sorenstam	Lidback	Bowen
1996	Davies	Sorenstam	Davies	Sheehan
1997	Johnson	Nicholas	Walker	King

Career Tournament Wins

1) Kathy Whitworth	88	11) Beth Daniel	32
2) Mickey Wright	82	12) Babe Zaharias	31
3) Patty Berg	57	Pat Bradley	31
4) Betsy Rawls	55	Betsy King	31
5) Louise Suggs	50	15) Amy Alcott	29
6) Nancy Lopez	48	Jane Blalock	29
7) JoAnne Carner	42	17) Judy Rankin	26
Sandra Haynie	42	18) Marlene Hagge	25
9) Carol Mann	38	19) Donna Caponi	24
10) Patty Sheehan	35	20) Marilynn Smith	22

Career Money Leaders

1) Betsy King	$5,980,113
2) Pat Bradley	5,539,184
3) Patty Sheehan	5,310,390
4) Beth Daniel	5,207,339
5) Nancy Lopez	5,008,521
6) Dottie Pepper	3,977,829
7) Laura Davies	3,626,879
8) Jane Geddes	3,305,616
9) Rosie Jones	3,276,833
10) Amy Alcott	3,261,334
11) Juli Inkster	3,083,805
12) Meg Mallon	3,046,591
13) JoAnne Carner	2,899,051
14) Annika Sorenstam	2,839,084
15) Tammie Green	2,803,295
16) Liselotte Neumann	2,793,109
17) Ayako Okamoto	2,743,174
18) Kelly Robbins	2,688,947
19) Chris Johnson	2,677,209
20) Colleen Walker	2,666,352

Annual Money Leaders

1950	Babe Zaharias	$14,800
1951	Babe Zaharias	15,087
1952	Betsy Rawls	14,505
1953	Louise Suggs	19,816
1954	Patty Berg	16,011
1955	Patty Berg	16,492
1956	Marlene Hagge	20,235
1957	Patty Berg	16,272
1958	Bevery Hanson	12,639
1959	Betsy Rawls	26,774
1960	Louise Suggs	16,892
1961	Mickey Wright	22,236

1962	Mickey Wright	$21,641
1963	Mickey Wright	31,269
1964	Mickey Wright	29,800
1965	Kathy Whitworth	28,658
1966	Kathy Whitworth	33,517
1967	Kathy Whitworth	32,937
1968	Kathy Whitworth	48,379
1969	Carol Mann	49,152
1970	Kathy Whitworth	30,235
1971	Kathy Whitworth	41,181
1972	Kathy Whitworth	65,063
1973	Kathy Whitworth	82,864
1974	JoAnne Carner	87,094
1975	Sandra Palmer	76,374
1976	Judy Rankin	150,734
1977	Judy Rankin	122,890
1978	Nancy Lopez	189,814
1979	Nancy Lopez	197,489
1980	Beth Daniel	231,000
1981	Beth Daniel	206,978
1982	JoAnne Carner	310,400
1983	JoAnne Carner	291,404
1984	Betsy King	266,771
1985	Nancy Lopez	416,472
1986	Pat Bradley	492,021
1987	Ayako Okamoto	466,034
1988	Sherri Turner	350,851
1989	Betsy King	654,132
1990	Beth Daniel	863,578
1991	Pat Bradley	763,118
1992	Dottie Mochrie	693,335
1993	Betsy King	595,992
1994	Laura Davies	687,201
1995	Annika Sorenstam	666,533
1996	Karrie Webb	1,002,000
1997	Annika Sorenstam	1,236,789

SENIOR PGA TOUR
Career Tournament Wins

1) Lee Trevino	27	Mike Hill	18
2) Miller Barber	24	9) George Archer	17
3) Bob Charles	23	10) Dave Stockton	14
4) Don January	22	11) Ray Floyd	13
Chi Chi Rodriguez	22	Hale Irwin	13
6) Bruce Crampton	20	12) Orville Moody	11
7) Gary Player	18	Peter Thomson	11

Career Tournament Wins (continued)

Dale Douglass	11	Jack Nicklaus	10
Jim Dent	11	Al Geiberger	10
Bob Murphy	11	20) Billy Casper	9
17) Arnold Palmer	10		

Career Money Leaders

1) Lee Trevino	$7,449,561
2) Bob Charles	7,244,675
3) Jim Colbert	7,126,797
4) Dave Stockton	6,636,029
5) Mike Hill	6,336,905
6) Chi Chi Rodriguez	6,068,903
7) George Archer	5,671,991
8) Raymond Floyd	5,580,271
9) Jim Dent	5,492,510
10) Dale Douglass	5,140,633
11) Isao Aoki	5,130,137
12) Hale Irwin	4,758,308
13) Bob Murphy	4,618,929
14) Gary Player	4,478,607
15) Bruce Crampton	4,391,178
16) Al Geiberger	4,103,795
17) J.C. Snead	4,023,511
18) Jim Albus	3,843,798
19) Miller Barber	3,800,297
20) Tom Wargo	3,670,425

Annual Money Leaders

1980	Don January	$44,000
1981	Miller Barber	83,136
1982	Miller Barber	106,890
1983	Don January	237,571
1984	Don January	328,597
1985	Peter Thomson	386,724
1986	Bruce Crampton	454,299
1987	Chi Chi Rodriguez	509,145
1988	Bob Charles	533,929
1989	Bob Charles	725,887
1990	Lee Trevino	1,190,518
1991	Mike Hill	1,065,657
1992	Lee Trevino	1,027,002
1993	Dave Stockton	1,175,944
1994	Dave Stockton	1,402,519
1995	Jim Colbert	1,444,386
1996	Jim Colbert	1,627,890
1997	Hale Irwin	2,343,364